The Sound of Tartini

Margherita Canale Degrassi and Paolo Da Col (eds.)

The Sound of Tartini

Instruments and Performing Practices in His Time

PETER LANG

Lausanne · Berlin · Bruxelles · Chennai · New York · Oxford

Library of Congress Cataloging-in-Publication Data
A CIP catalog record for this book has been applied for at the
Library of Congress.

Bibliographic information published by the Deutsche Nationalbibliothek.
The German National Library lists this publication in the German National
Bibliography; detailed bibliographic data is available on the Internet
at http://dnb.d-nb.de.

This volume was published with the support of the Centre of Tartini's studies
Centro di Documentazione e Studi Tartiniani "Bruno e Michèle Polli" of the
Music Conservatory "Giuseppe Tartini" of Trieste.

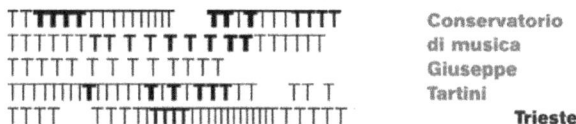

Conservatorio
di musica
Giuseppe
Tartini
Trieste

Cover illustration:
Violin bridge belonged to Tartini, in maple wood, 18th century (Trieste,
Conservatorio Giuseppe Tartini)
Portrait of G. Tartini, tempera on paper, second half of 18th century (Trieste,
Conservatorio Giuseppe Tartini)

ISBN 978-3-631-87490-5 (Print)
E-ISBN 978-3-631-89477-4 (E-PDF)
E-ISBN 978-3-631-89478-1 (E-PUB)
10.3726/b20468

© 2023 Peter Lang Group AG, Lausanne
Published by Peter Lang GmbH, Berlin, Deutschland

info@peterlang.com - www.peterlang.com

Table of Contents

Tartini's Sound Legacy: Stylistic Influences, Interpretation and Performing Practice

List of Contributors

Antonino Airenti
Independent scholar, luthier and professional bowmaker specialized in the repro-
duction of historical bows

Alfredo Bernardini
Mozarteum University, Salzburg

Federico Gon
Conservatorio "Giuseppe Tartini", Trieste

Johannes Loescher MA (Magister Artium)
Violin maker, musician and musicologist

Domen Marinčič
Hochschule für Musik und Theater Hamburg

Dario Marušić
Independent musician, expert in Istrian folk music

Donatella Melini
Pavia University

Federica Nuvoli
Conservatorio "Luigi Canepa", Sassari

Marc Vanscheeuwijck
University of Oregon – Conservatoire Royal de Bruxelles

Preface

The last few years have seen important occasions to revisit the life and work of the famous violinist, composer, music teacher and music theorist Giuseppe Tartini (1692–1770): 2020 was the 250th anniversary of his death and 2022 was the 330th anniversary of his birth. To mark the occasion, the Department of Linguistic and Literary Studies of the University of Padua, the Department of Musicology of the Faculty of Arts, University of Ljubljana and the "Giuseppe Tartini" Conservatory in Trieste joined forces and organized three international musicological conferences between 2019 and 2020, exploring topics related to Tartini's life, work and legacy. The present three-volume series, *Giuseppe Tartini and the Musical Culture of Enlightenment*, edited by Margherita Canale Degrassi, Paolo Da Col, Nejc Sukljan, and Gabriele Taschetti, presents a thematically organized selection of the expanded and revised conference papers. In these years, the Conservatorio di Musica di Trieste (duly named after great musician born in Piran in Istria in 1692) has contributed to the study of Giuseppe Tartini's life and music within the framework of the important Italy-Slovenia Interreg project *tARTini* (2014–20). The school has not only offered musicological counselling but also promoted the digitalization of musical sources and historical documents, the performance of unpublished music, the digital development of the composer's thematic catalogue, the creation of a museum of "Tartini Relics" with a virtual tour, recordings and research (https://www.discovertartini.eu/). One of the most significant events of the project was the International Conference "Il suono di Tartini" held in Trieste on 6 and 7 September 2019, whose contributions are here included in this volume. A theme of the conference, which is duly reflected in this volume, was to encourage the union of musicological research and interpretation, and the collaboration between scholar and performer, musicologist and musician.

The rediscovery and reassessment of Tartini must indeed pass through the "practical" research of performers. Many issues, which emerge in performance, are resolved by the interpreter engaged with the concrete business of reviving the performing context of the age. The common thread running through these studies is therefore the search for the "Tartini sound": to recover the ensembles used in his age, the constructional features of the instruments, the materials of which they were made, and their characteristic sound and timbre, and to offer a reconstruction of that sound world and idea of music by drawing on the period's attitude to matters of performance, interpretation and expression. Tartini's musical world presented various important and original features. His contemporaries saw a distinct consistency in the stylistic ideals and interpretational tastes of those working in his circle, associating them with a vocal and discursive approach to music. Significantly, many statements made by Tartini in his letters and theoretical works refer to the art of "singing" on the violin: a manner of singing that depends on the movements of the bow and the inflections of phrasing, which, again according to

Tartini, must follow the "sense" of the melody, as if it were some kind of discourse. This is the performing style acknowledged to be a characteristic of his school and, as such, also attributed to an important musician of that circle: the cellist Antonio Vandini, Tartini's faithful friend, who (according to the musicologist Burney, who heard him play) "plays [...] in such a manner as to make his instrument *speak*".

This third volume of the series "*Giuseppe Tartini and the Musical Culture of the Enlightenment*" carries the title *The Sound of Tartini: Instruments and Performing practices in His Time*. It focuses first of all on analysing the evidence concerning instrument building and sound research relating to Tartini and his circle; then it goes on to look at the personalities of his musician colleagues and examine information on performances at the *cappella* of the Basilica del Santo in Padua; and finally it concludes with matters concerning Tartini's influence on later musicians.

After Sergio Durante's opening article, which summarizes the current state of play on the performance of Tartini's music and musicological research, this volume is divided into three sections.

The first section, *The Production of Sound: Instruments and Bows in Tartini's Time*, is introduced by a wide-ranging article by Donatella Melini that examines the evolution of the bow in the stringed instruments of Tartini's day through comprehensive research into the iconographic, theoretical and historical sources. Johannes Loescher assesses Italian instrument-making at the time of Tartini, and in particular the *Regole* of the Paduan instrument maker Antonio Airenti, in connection with the violin fittings preserved among the "Tartini relics", while Antonino Airenti tackles the issue of reconstructing the type of sound that can be obtained from those surviving relics.

The second section, *The Sound Environment at the Basilica del Santo di Padova: Colleagues and Orchestra*, focuses both on certain musical personalities with whom Tartini was in close contact at the orchestra of the Basilica and on certain aspects relating to the performing customs at the *cappella*. While Marc Vanscheeuwijck presents the cello though the personality and work of Antonio Vandini, cellist, colleague and friend of Tartini, Alfredo Bernardini investigates the life and work of the oboist Matteo Bissoli, also working in Padua in Tartini's day. Domen Marinčič, availing himself of various contemporary sources, studies aspects of performance practice and explores the possibility of performing Tartini's works (including the orchestral pieces) without the accompaniment of keyboard instruments.

The third section, *Tartini's Sound Legacy: Stylistic Influences, Interpretation and Performing Practice*, rounds off the volume first with an article by Federica Nuvoli, who presents the influence of Tartini on the work of Domenico Dall'Oglio, a Paduan violinist who worked at the court of Empress Catherine in Russia. Next, Federico Gon tackles aspects of violin technique such as *bariolage* in the production of Joseph Haydn, conjecturing that the composer working at Esterházy could have been influenced by the activities of Tartini's pupils. This section concludes with the article by Dario Marušić on the tradition of folk music for strings in Istria and its ties with the Baroque repertoire, while leaving open the hypotheses on the possible links between Tartini and these repertoires.

We hope that this volume may contribute to opening up further lines of research and, moreover, be of interest to those wishing to approach the versatile and fascinating personality of Giuseppe Tartini in different ways, studying him from the historical, musicological or interpretative points of view, as well as being useful to those interested in the history of taste, style and customs.

Margherita Canale Degrassi
Editor

Sergio Durante

University of Padua

The Tartini Moment

It is in the mindset of musicologists to consider performance the conclusion of a process that originates from a careful consideration of the sources, be they historical documents or properly musical texts. In the case of Tartini, however, the contrary might be honestly said: performers arrived before scholars and offered to their audiences, both in concert and in recordings, direct and effective musical experiences, notwithstanding that the scores in use were not necessarily up to the scholarly standard. We must then recognize that it is mainly the merit of practical musicians if Tartini is better known today than it was 30 years ago. A number of new recordings appeared before and/or in connection with the Tartini year 2020, marking a resurgence that is particularly noteworthy insofar as it does not depend on joint planning, on a major festival or institution but on the individual initiatives of performers. It is not only the quality of first-class performers in play but also the diverse concepts enlivening the projects. This is not the occasion for a complete discography, but at least a selection of cases must be mentioned: in the first place the complete recording of the violin concertos published by Dynamic, a huge enterprise planned and achieved over the years with unmeasurable determination, energy and competence by the late Giovanni Guglielmo, his son Federico and Carlo Lazari with period instruments ensemble *L'arte dell'arco*.[1] The fact of making available to the public 125 concertos in 29 CDs represents a turn in Tartini's reception. After the edition was completed, new concertos by (or attributed to) Tartini surfaced, thanks to researchers, but I suspect that a part of the newly found 30 works will need a prudent assessment of authenticity since the "Tartini" label encouraged forgery as was the case with other eighteenth-century-celebrated masters.[2] Another interesting collection of 13 CDs encloses all of Enrico Gatti's sonata recordings and nests the reprint of sonatas Op. I (Le Cène, 1734, the most circulated collection throughout Europe) and Op. II (Clèton, 1745, the only Italian print); this collection represents not only a homage to one brilliant violinist in historically informed performance but, more importantly, places Tartini within a frame of contemporary composers that stresses his peculiarity. Projects of lesser magnitude are equally important in that they offer original approaches to a music style that is appreciated more and more as its profundity is understood: David Plantier has published (with Annabelle

---

1 Giuseppe Tartini, *The Violin concertos (Complete) (box set)*, L'arte dell'arco, Dynamic CDS7713, 2015, CD.

2 On the sources for the solo concertos see Margherita Canale Degrassi, "The Solo Concertos by Giuseppe Tartini: Sources, Tradition and Thematic Catalogue," *Ad Parnassum* 11, no. 22 (2013): 11–49.

Luis, cello) various recordings in what is probably the phonic arrangement closest to the Paduan practice of the time, that is, with cello solo rather than cello and harpsichord.[3] The result is fully convincing for the emerging clarity of the contrapuntal texture no less than for the instrumental quality and interpretive sensibility. This apparently radical, certainly untraditional choice, anticipates and matches recent investigations of the sources (without, of course, excluding the possibility of a more traditional performance *à tre*). One of Plantier's CDs is based on the careful use of the ms. FR-Pc 9796, and is devoted to Tartini's last violin sonatas: the source itself directs the artist towards the choice of demonstrably late works of top quality, side by side with the early sonata D19. Yet another original approach is represented by Mathieu Camilleri CD titled *Senti lo mare* (Listen to the Sea), one of the literary incipits chosen by Tartini as "creative prompter":[4] besides offering a stylistically convincing performance, the artist aims at reviving the improvisational *manière* by Tartini offering, besides diminutions and embellishments, a *Prélude/Capriccio* entirely original, and yet shaped according to the long-internalized style of Tartini. Among the artists who are presently demonstrating a special interest for the piranese virtuoso, one should not forget Marie Rouquié, Leila Schayegh and Chouchane Siranossian,[5] protagonists of diverse but equally convincing renderings of Tartini's music. Of course, one should not neglect the gratitude due to violinists of the old school, among whom Piero Toso, Uto Ughi, Salvatore Accardo and others, but I feel that only in the vast and yet diverse region of historically informed practices, the peculiar greatness of Tartini will become fully transparent. This does not represent advocacy of a movement that does not need any but, more simply, the consequence of considering the foundations of Tartini's fortune in his time, no less than his substantial oblivion during the nineteenth and most of the twentieth centuries. First and more obviously he was a performer of exceptional skill who invented devices for the use of his instrument, sound combinations and effects that appeared new and surprising. His mastery of the bow, on one hand, and his expressive sound production, on the other, appeared unprecedented to contemporary listeners. We can only imagine the quality of that impression 250 years after the facts, but Tartini himself provides a clue about the indispensable relation between *his* compositions and a specific style of performance. In 1749 he was commissioned a number of compositions by Frederick the Great through Francesco Algarotti, and on the occasion, he cautioned his intermediary about the risks (in a letter of 20 November 1749):

---

3   Giuseppe Tartini, *Cantabile e suonabile*, Duo Tartini: David Plantier, Annabelle Luis, AgOgique AGO020, 2015, CD; Giuseppe Tartini, *Continuo addio!*, Duo Tartini: David Plantier, Annabelle Luis, Muso MU-031, 2019, CD; Giuseppe Tartini, *Vertigo (The Last Violin Sonatas)*, Duo Tartini: David Plantier, Annabelle Luis, Muso MU-040, 2020, CD.

4   Giuseppe Tartini, *Senti lo mare. Sonates pour violon seul*, Matthieu Camilleri, En Phases, ENP002, 2018, CD.

5   See her recordings of five concertos, including a first performance, in Giuseppe Tartini, *Tartini: Violin Concertos*, Chouchane Siranossian, Venice Baroque Orchestra, Andrea Marcon, Alpha ALPHA596, 2020, CD.

[...] I must inform you (as a good servant) to limit my praises with this marvelous monarch. As on the one hand he is too wise in every matter, and on the other your love for me exceeds any merit and any talent of mine. And although this love is very dear and most precious to me, I could never allow it to be harmful to such a patron of mine, as could easily happen in the present case, in which I am obliged by your command to send my compositions there to be examined and judged by this monarch. I blindly obey you, as I shall always do, but may God assist you. The gamble in the performance adds to this, since it is equally as impossible that another man (whoever he may be) might match my character and my expression with precision, as it is impossible for another man to look exactly like me.[6]

We have no way to know whether Frederick liked the pieces or not, but he was kind enough to Tartini with an original melody that was then used as a theme for a new concerto.[7] The text stresses the crucial importance of adequate performance and conversely that, in absence of such, the composer himself could raise doubts about the outcome. After Tartini died and his compositional style became old-fashioned, most of his music fell in oblivion for a long time. This does not diminish the value of Tartini's compositions but calls for a suitable approach: this music needs an eloquent, superior performance or, in other words, as Giulio Caccini wrote "non patisce mediocrità" (does not suffer mediocrity). One should add that it does not suffer equal temperament, poor intonation, constant vibrato and lack of

---

6   "[...] devo avvertirla (come buon servitore) a misurar le mie lodi con cotesto maraviglioso monarca. Perché da una parte egli è troppo veggente in ogni genere, e dall'altra il di lei amore verso di me eccede qualunque merito, e qualunque mia dote. E sebbene questo amore mi è carissimo, e pretiosissimo non potrò mai permettere che al un tale e tanto mio padrone, riesca dannoso, come può facilmente succedere nel caso presente in cui dal di lei comando sono obbligato mandar costà le mie compositioni all'esame e giudicio di cotesto monarca. Io la obedisco ciecamente, come la obedirò sempre, ma Dio gliela mandi buona. Vi si aggiunge l'azzardo della essecutione: essendo egualmente impossibile che un altro uomo (qualunque sia) incontri di punto il mio carattere, e la mia espressione, com'è impossibile, che un altro uomo perfettamente mi rassomigli." Giorgia Malagò, ed., *Giuseppe Tartini: Lettere e documenti/Pisma in dokumenti/Letters and Documents*, trans. Jerneja Umer Kljun and Roberto Baldo, vol. 1 (Trieste: Edizioni Università di Trieste, 2020): 179. English translation in Malagò, *Tartini: Lettere*, 2:318. For a bibliographical survey on Tartini up to 2013 see Sergio Durante, "Tartini Studies: The State of the Art," *Ad Parnassum* 11, no. 22 (2013): 1–10.

7   This is reported in Francesco Fanzago, *Orazione del signor abate Francesco Fanzago padovano delle lodi di Giuseppe Tartini* [...] *con un breve compendio della vita del medesimo* (Padova: Stamperia Conzatti, 1770), 19; and in Sergio Durante, *Tartini, Padova, l'Europa* (Livorno: Le Sillabe 2017), 85; and represents a parallel to the *soggetto reale* presented to J.S. Bach. Both composers built on the king's gift a full-size work (or set of works), but unfortunately we have presently no clues leading to the identification of Tartini's one.

clarity. If it is true that (some) performers understood this first, the time has come for musicologists to provide musicians with critical editions of Tartini's oeuvre, amounting to approximately 420 catalogue numbers according to the most recent count.[8]

However, in order to provide an orientation within this massive musical and theoretical output, we also need a more detailed, and perhaps less eulogistic, narration about Tartini's life and ideas. Pierluigi Petrobelli, the most important Tartini scholar of the twentieth century, believed in the image of Giuseppe as a "totally honest" man,[9] but I would suggest that we inherited rather uncritically Tartini's self-representation while a reliable portrait of any personality must be more complicated and contradictory. Tartini's reputation was in reality not only the result of a candid devotion to music but also of a forward-looking career planning. He was hired at St Anthony's basilica in 1721, and with the exception of the three Prague years (1723–1726), he played there until his retirement in 1765 (30–35 performances each year). Not enough attention has been paid so far to the uniqueness of that position: how many violinists became the main musical attraction of a major sanctuary for the fascination of instrumental performance (and not of their liturgical compositions)? None to my knowledge. By staying in Padua, rather than accepting the more prestigious positions that he was repeatedly offered, Tartini was assuring to himself a composite audience not only of local population but also, much more importantly, of wealthy travellers on their *Grand tour* who became as many advertisers of their privileged musical experience at St Anthony's. When Burney reported in his *Musical travel through Italy* that he visited Padua with the attitude of "a pilgrim to Mecca" (months after Tartini's death), he was characterizing the city as a music-shrine and Tartini (rather than St Anthony) as the object of veneration: the overlapping of sanctuary and music venue was perfect in his imagination as it had been successfully functional to Tartini's international image.[10]

It is not far-fetched to say that, consciously or not (I believe consciously), Tartini devised a lucid planning: not by chance his first book of concertos was published in Amsterdam in 1726 or 1727, immediately after the opening in Padua of the school of violin and composition that was to become his main source of income. According to the report of Achilles Rhyner-Delon (and implicitly by the over 100 students who attended his lessons), he was a careful, charismatic and

---

8   The new thematic catalogue of Tartini has been realized with the support of the EU Interreg ITA-SLO. See Guido Viverit, Alba Luksich, and Simone Olivari, eds., "Catalogo tematico delle composizioni di Giuseppe Tartini," *Discover Tartini, tARTini-Turismo culturale all'insegna di Giuseppe Tartini Interreg ITA–SLO*, 2019–2020, http://catalog.discovertartini.eu/dcm/gt/navigation.xq.

9   This is a literal quote from personal discussions I had in the autumn of 2011 with Petrobelli; he probably derived this persuasion both from the eulogistic text of Fanzago and from his readings of the letters.

10 Read in the edition, Charles Burney, *Viaggio musicale in Italia*, trans. Enrico Fubini (Torino: EDT, 1979), 123.

effective teacher;[11] however, his special teaching talent is not a sufficient explanation: opening a private school that attracted students from all over the continent (and beyond) was also a form of self-promotion. Some of them were exceptionally good, like Bini, Pagin or Nardini; many more were wealthy amateurs of diverse proficiency, all equally eager to boast of their studies with Tartini, all trumpeting his virtuosity and his techniques, as witnessed in E.T.A. Hoffmann's tale recently reprinted as *L'allievo di Tartini* (Tartini's student).[12]

Even the too often repeated story of the devil's dream, reappraised from the psychoanalytical perspective by Roberta Guarnieri,[13] can be seen with new eyes: what was for Tartini the use of insisting in the narration of that story? If we believe de Lalande's report, the dream was the stimulus for the composition of a piece that he reputed "his best and yet inferior to the one heard in the dream";[14] we must also recall that, according to the visitor Christoph Gottlieb von Murr, a score of the *Devil's Trill sonata* was hanging at the wall of the room where Tartini taught,[15] like an emblem of his inspiration. The story of the dream must have been told time and again (as proved by its synthetic and variant version in Cartier's l'*Art du violon*).[16] We might then argue, with a degree of cynicism, that Tartini was using his dream as yet another element of self-mythography, possibly delineating a marketing strategy *avant-lettre*.[17] Therefore, he might have been an honest man, in his own way, but he was neither a saint nor indifferent to finances or to artistic and intellectual glory.

---

11 Martin Staehelin, "Giuseppe Tartini über seine künstlerische Entwicklung," *Archiv für Musikwissenschaft*, no. 35 (1978): 251–274.

12 The original title was *Der Baron von B.* (1818–1819). See Ernst Theodor Amadeus Hoffman, *L'allievo di Tartini ed altri racconti musicali* (Firenze: Passigli 1984), 103–119.

13 See Roberta Guarnieri, "Tartini and the Psychoanalyst: dream and musical creation," in *Giuseppe Tartini: Fundamental Questions*, ed. Gabriele Taschetti (Berlin: Peter Lang, 2022), 143–148.

14 Joseph Jérôme de Lalande, *Voyage d'un françois en Italie dans les années 1765 et 1766*, vol. 8 (Paris, 1769), 292–294.

15 Pierluigi Petrobelli, *Giuseppe Tartini: Le fonti biografiche* (Venice: Universal, 1968), 78–79; the visit must have taken place around 1760.

16 The caption of the devil "a pié del letto" (at the bed's foot) is a representation that differs from de Lalande's narration and introduces a third implicit protagonist, the reader who imagines Tartini dreaming in his sleep: the tale leaps from the subjective (Tartinian) perspective and is objectified. See Jean-Baptiste Cartier, *L'art du violon* (Paris: Decombe, 1803).

17 It is significant that Michele Stratico, one of Tartini's best students, left a manuscript dissertation titled *Lo spirito tartiniano* ("Lo spirito Tartiniano," by Michele Stratico, fols. 171–191, I-Vnm, Ms. It. Cl. IV, 343e [= 5348], National Library "Marciana", Venice), in which he imagines a fictitious dream and a discussion on music theory with his late master: the oniric dimension left evidently a mark in the *School of the nations*.

The historical investigation on Tartini leads us into regions that are unusual for a standard violinist of the mid-eighteenth century or, as he belittlingly liked to define himself, a "segatore di violino".[18] This "violin sawyer" was in reality a man of the highest ambitions that originated both from his natural talents and from his upbringing. Being the son of an important civil servant and member of a prominent family in Piran, he was expected from childhood to aim at a social status that could not be attained through the profession of music. Also, his achievements in music theory, mistakenly considered in the literature as a replacement for performance and composition in his late years, might be seen more convincingly as a psychological compensation of his social downgrading from the élite – where his family needed him to be – to the lower guild of practical musicians. While this interpretation is logical, it is also incomplete and in part unfair: the study of his epistolary shows that the passion for intellectual exercises of different sorts was alive since childhood and surfaced in diverse fields and different moments of his life: the early letters of 1731 to Giovanni Battista Martini, a younger and not yet famous colleague at the time, demonstrate interest for the art of enigmatic canons (the traditionally "higher craft" of composition). In 1741 he tried to convince Martini and through him Paolo Battista Balbi of having solved important mathematical problems. At a later stage, around 1751, his focus became the prestigious riddle of squaring the circle: he tried through Francesco Algarotti and the Venetian *doge* Pietro Grimani to obtain recognition (and possibly a dedication) from Frederick of Prussia. Then came his treatise of 1754 *Trattato di musica secondo la vera scienza dell'armonia* (Treatise on Music according to the True Science of Harmony) that can be seen from two different perspectives: it is in part a treatise on music through which Tartini assesses the physical and mathematical foundations of his art (conceived essentially as the combination of melody and harmony in relation to a diatonic scale defined by nature); it is also an attempt to provide and demonstrate a link between physics and metaphysics. In the second chapter, he explains to his noble student, Decio Agostino Trento:

> [...] I can praise myself of being perhaps the first (at least in present times) to discover the metaphysics of quantitative sciences, deducted from physical facts in such a way that it is impossible to separate them. I follow the truth which is found within the things, as far as it leads me; I am sure to have proceeded rigorously up to the present day. And so will I do until the end.[19]

---

18 Letter to P. B. Balbi of April 14, 1741. See Malagò, *Tartini: Lettere* 1:150.
19 "[...] posso tenermi in pregio di esser forse il primo (almeno in questi tempi) che scuopra la metafisica delle scienze di quantità, dedotta dalle cose fisiche in tal modo, che sia impossibile il separarla. Seguo il vero, ch'è nelle cose, fin dove mi conduce; e son certo di averlo fin'ora seguito a tutto rigore. Così farò fino alla fine." Giuseppe Tartini, *Trattato di musica secondo la vera scienza dell'armonia* (Padova: Stamperia del Seminario, 1754), 32. English translation by the author.

This quite-unheard-of goal is very telling of Tartini's excessive intellectual ambition.[20] Was it the disproportionate consequence of a mentally unbalanced personality, of senility perhaps? The answer is more complex. We must recall that in his cultural context the connection between the science of sound and that of number descended from a long tradition reflected, with different outcomes, in Jean Philippe Rameau's theoretical works. In other words, if a musician tried to elevate his craft to the level of science, the effort had to focus on the so-called *historia naturalis* (science of nature) rather than on the crono-historical, anthropological or linguistic plan.

One of the troubles in the approach to Tartini's theoretical writings comes from the impression of obscurity – in reality dissolved by Patrizio Barbieri in his numerous writings[21] – and of their idleness with respect to its applicability to practice. But the application to music practice was not at all the main preoccupation of the author: we must realize that the notion of "music theory" as it came to be elaborated in the nineteenth and twentieth centuries has little to do with Tartini's (or Rameau's) purposes. The cultural limits of the time provided as many straitjackets to their investigations. Two in particular need mention: eurocentrism and the related idea that the music of their time had achieved a degree of perfection as never before. As a consequence the investigation of music as language did not question the inherited principle of the *numero senario* (representing the natural legitimation of the intervals in current use) nor took into deep consideration the theoretical consequences of the upper harmonic pitches so that their sight was self-limited to the "nature" of lower harmonics (the theoretically more convenient 5th and 3rd).[22] In the end the theoretical process aimed almost by necessity to the discovery of the originating principle of harmony, be it the fundamental bass (for Rameau) or the third tone (for Tartini). This so-called "theory" did not extend to, nor explain, the existing musical objects but rather collapsed on itself. The extreme consequence of this conceptual loop is the treatise *Scienza platonica fondata nel cerchio* (Platonic Science Founded in the Circle) where Tartini tried to reconnect all the steps of his intellectual development: the empirical investigation

---

20 See also Sergio Durante, "Giuseppe Tartini nella rete dei *savants*," in *Padua als Europäisches Wissenschaftszentrum von der Renaissance bis zur Aufklärung*, ed. Dietrich von Engelhardt, Gian Franco Frigo (Aachen: Shaker, 2017), 195–204; Sergio Durante, "Lungo il solco tracciato: esperienza acustiche e riflessioni estetiche da Galileo a Tartini," *Atti e memorie dell'Accademia galileiana di scienze, lettere ed arti* (2016–2017): 33–42.

21 See, in particular, Patrizio Barbieri, *Acustica, accordatura e temperamento nell'Illuminismo Veneto* (Rome: Torre d'Orfeo, 1987); and the fundamental Patrizio Barbieri, *Quarrels on harmonic theories in the Venetian Enlightenment* (Lucca: LIM, 2020).

22 For the meaning of *senario* and the relevance of the lower harmonics in eighteenth-century music theories, see Barbieri, *Quarrels*, and Sergio Durante, "Giuseppe Tartini nella rete dei savants".

of combination tones, their arithmetical consequences on pitch relations, and their supposed ties to Plato's writings (at the origin of Western culture) and far back to Hermes Trismegistos,[23] whose "fragments" were discredited for many by the mid-eighteenth century but still valuable for Tartini.

The scholar is tempted to dismiss this whole field as irrelevant for the purpose of music history: after all our focus and interest is Tartini's compositional output while speculations bordering with hermetic philosophy will lead us nowhere, as much as they led the aging Tartini to frustration and conflict. However, this is only half true because, from a different vantage point, those ideas represent the intimate persuasion of a creative artist and, within such limits, they are precious evidence of an aesthetical and ethical outlook that supported the art works we investigate today. In sum, assuming that Tartini's speculations are irrelevant to his music is even less convincing than his metaphysical intuitions, not intended after all to development but to coincide with his intense and somewhat anguished catholic faith. On the larger canvas Tartini's theories can be seen as a significant if underrated episode in the intellectual history of the mid-eighteenth century, illustrating a possibly darker side of the Enlightenment and at the same time representing evidence of the inherent contradictions of that time and culture. Tartini's speculations, in sum, add to our understanding of the broader European culture while providing material for a truthful investigation of the artist's mindset.

The collective effort that characterizes the current scholarly interest in Tartini faces tasks that concern not only the assessment of one composer's output but also shed light on the age. In the first place we should get rid of what I might call the "baroque" misunderstanding: since this term came to be applied with substantial superficiality to music, composers, musical instruments of the period until 1760 or even later, it finally came to mean nothing. We should refrain from applying it to Tartini or to any of the styles and/or personalities that consciously adhered to the anti-baroque ideals of the Enlightenment (to what degree the Enlightenment realized its ideals is of course another question). Once we take this step, it will be easy to see the diverse and non-directional multiplicity of styles and individual aesthetic attitudes coexisting at the time. In the past, the value of Tartini's music has been supported by considering him a link towards Classicism, or a Pre-romantic personality: none of the above is necessary nor true, but reflects the attitude to represent history as an orderly, teleological, linear process: it is more complicated than that. We might ask, conversely, how we should represent Tartini's "case" within the tangle of European music, the intricate overlapping of social and institutional macro-structures: that of the temples, courts and scriptoria, characterized by higher stability and that of the commercial theatres, concert venues, music prints characterized by circulation of artists and repertories. In that intricate old-régime reality Tartini realized an intermediate and original professional pattern, his own personal style and his own repertory.

***

---

23 Malagò, *Tartini: Lettere*, 1:186.

If it is true, as stated in the beginning, that performers arrived first, it is now time to provide them with reliable editions of the approximately 420 opus numbers. If we look at Tartini's oeuvre at a distance, we realize the complexity of the enterprise because, in a sense, he composed too much music in too few genres and without caring to date them, generating one of the most intricate chronology riddles. At least some of his most important prints were authorized and provide a chronological frame for the early- to mid-life production. These are all the works published by Michel Charles Le Cène: the 17 concertos of Op. I, books 1–3, to be considered significant early works; his 19 sonatas of Op. I (1734) and Op. II (the penultimate print by Le Cène, completed after his death in 1743), the 12 *Sonatas* (also as Op. II) printed in Rome by Cléton (1745). This accounts for 17 concertos (24 if we tentatively add the Witvogel editions) and 31 sonatas over a total of 161 and 204, respectively (one set of Trio sonatas printed in London "at the author expense" in 1750 is in doubt of authenticity). Tartini considered at least two more publication projects for concertos (12 and 6, respectively) and one set of sonatas, but they never materialized. It is impossible to say why but I surmise that there were sufficient works by Tartini on the market by the mid-eighteenth century (both authorized and not), at a point in his career when he was famous and his teaching earned him more money than any new print would. It is noteworthy that he kept composing until his last years, contrary to the traditional notion that he abandoned composition in favour of music theory. Of this huge heritage only a fraction is available today in reliable editions: we must be grateful to Edoardo Farina and Claudio Scimone for their editorial work in the 1970s, without which almost no Tartini music would be circulating,[24] but it must be stressed that the only truly critical edition available today is Agnese Pavanello's *Devil's Trill* sonata (Brainard g5) published by Bärenreiter. The next step will be Tartini's *Opera omnia*, a difficult yet overdue enterprise that confronts one of the most intricate transmissions.[25] Despite the current expansion of research we are not yet in the position to have a complete grasp of his stylistic development, except for the valuable but too general characterizations by Dounias and Brainard. We will certainly know more as the patient work of text criticism for the new edition is carried forward, but this will take time. In the while, a few impressions on characteristic aspects are in order. The form of Tartini's compositions is stable to the point of letting us suspect his indifference to formal invention as such. In concertos the *ritornello form* remains basically unvaried through his career with few exceptions (e.g. the concerto for Lunardo Venier); in sonatas he adopts almost exclusively the binary form or rarely

---

24 A reconsideration is found in Sergio Durante, "Il contributo di Claudio Scimone alla conoscenza di Giuseppe Tartini," in *Claudio Scimone (1934–2018). Contributi per una storicizzazione*, ed. Sergio Durante and Claudio Griggio (Firenze: Olschki, 2021), 27–35.

25 The first volume of the series is due in 2022 and represents a completely new edition of *L'arte dell'arco*, ed. Matteo Cossu and published by Bärenreiter.

the variation (possibly a relic of the final *ciaccona*). In mainstream musicological tradition this leads to a negative aesthetical evaluation, but it may suggest instead that the value of this music must be searched elsewhere. It would be misleading to expect a renovation or complication of forms: if anything, the contrary is true and can be seen in his relatively late "little sonatas", traditionally identified with the pieces (or part of them) transmitted in the important autograph I-Pca, 1888. Here not only the standard movement is short but also the performing medium tends to a minimum, renouncing the accompaniment of the bass while entrusting its function to the double stops of the cello or to the underlying (and more "theoretical" than actually audible) third tone. In this we might read a trend towards simplification or even aphoristic form, coherent on one hand with the idea that the kernel of compositional application is the primary melodic invention and its aural (i.e. timbral) articulation, and on the other with the practical use of such pieces, probably intended by Tartini for private use in solo performances (and in fact never published in his lifetime). Tartini's concept of form as a simple functional frame rather than object of invention is also clear in the concertos. The potential monotony of this approach is balanced in the fast movements by the unending inventiveness of thematic gestures and by the progressive technical complication of the solo sections delineating a climactic, elementary, additive structure. The essentially virtuosic poetics of the fast movements is not denied but balanced by the intense expressivity of the slow ones where Tartini's originality of ethos and *Stimmung* comes to the fore. If this reading is correct, I find all the more dubious to recognize Tartini's concerto style as a step towards Classicism, and even less towards Romanticism on account of his demonstrably "sentimental" aesthetics,[26] unless this reference is meant in its most generic terms.

A lot has been done in the past 40 years and more is happening today in Tartini's research, but the vast continent of Tartini's music remains superficially explored or, more optimistically, is in the process of laborious analysis, a collective task entrusted to a new generation of scholars and to their willingness to explain and narrate the connections between the many facets of an intriguing personality: the man, the violinist, the composer, the scientist, the enlightened prophet of music science.

Bibliography

Barbieri, Patrizio. *Acustica, accordatura e temperamento nell'illuminismo veneto. Con scritti inediti di Alessandro Barca, Giordano Riccati e altri autori.* Roma: Torre d'Orfeo, 1987.

Barbieri, Patrizio. *Quarrels on harmonic theories in the Venetian Enlightenment.* Lucca: LIM, 2020.

---

26 On this see Pierpaolo Polzonetti, *Tartini e la musica secondo natura* (Lucca: LIM, 2001).

Burney, Charles. *Viaggio musicale in Italia.* Translated by Enrico Fubini. Torino: EDT, 1979.

Canale, Margherita. "The Solo Concertos by Giuseppe Tartini: Sources, Tradition and Thematic Catalogue." *Ad Parnassum* 11, no. 22 (2013): 11–49.

Cartier, Jean-Baptiste. *L'art du violon.* Paris: Decombe, 1803.

Durante, Sergio. "Giuseppe Tartini nella rete dei *savants.*" In *Padua als Europäisches Wissenschaftszentrum von der Renaissance bis zur Aufklärung,* edited by Dietrich von Engelhardt and Gian Franco Frigo, 195–204. Aachen: Shaker, 2017.

Durante, Sergio. "Tartini Studies: The State of the Art." *Ad Parnassum* 11, no. 22 (2013): 1–10.

Durante, Sergio. "Lungo il solco tracciato: esperienza acustiche e riflessioni estetiche da Galileo a Tartini." *Atti e memorie dell'Accademia galileiana di scienze, lettere ed arti* (2016–2017): 33–42.

Durante, Sergio. *Tartini, Padova, L'Europa.* Livorno: Le Sillabe, 2017.

Durante, Sergio. "Il contributo di Claudio Scimone alla conoscenza di Giuseppe Tartini." In *Claudio Scimone (1934–2018). Contributi per una storicizzazione,* edited by Sergio Durante and Claudio Griggio, 27–35. Firenze: Olschki, 2021.

Fanzago, Francesco. *Orazione del signor abate Francesco Fanzago padovano delle lodi di Giuseppe Tartini recitata nella chiesa de' rr. pp. Serviti in Padova li 31. marzo l'anno 1770. Con varie note illustrata, e con un breve compendio della vita del medesimo.* Padova: Stamperia Conzatti, 1770.

Guarnieri, Roberta. "Tartini and the Psychoanalyst: dream and musical creation." In *Giuseppe Tartini: Fundamental Questions,* edited by Gabriele Taschetti, 143–148. Berlin: Peter Lang, 2022.

Hoffmann, Ernst Theodor Amadeus. *L'allievo di Tartini ed altri racconti musicali.* Firenze: Passigli 1984.

Lalande, Joseph Jérôme. *Voyage d'un français en Italie dans les années 1765 et 1766,* vol. 8. Paris: n.p., 1769.

Malagò, Giorgia, ed. *Giuseppe Tartini: Lettere e documenti/Pisma in dokumenti/ Letters and Documents.* 2 vols. Translated by Jerneja Umer Kljun and Roberto Baldo. Trieste: Edizioni Università di Trieste, 2020.

Petrobelli, Pierluigi. *Giuseppe Tartini: Le fonti biografiche.* Venice-Vienna: Universal, 1968.

Polzonetti, Pierpaolo. *Tartini e la musica secondo natura.* Lucca: LIM, 2001.

Staehelin, Martin. "Giuseppe Tartini über seine künstlerische Entwicklung." *Archiv für Musikwissenschaft* 35 (1978): 251–274.

Stratico, Michele. "Lo spirito Tartiniano." Fols. 171–191, I-Vnm, Ms. It. Cl. IV, 343e [= 5348], National Library "Marciana", Venice.

Tartini, Giuseppe. *Trattato di musica secondo la vera scienza dell'armonia.* Padova: Stamperia del Seminario, 1754.

Viverit, Guido, Alba Luksich, Simone Olivari, eds. "Catalogo tematico delle composizioni di Giuseppe Tartini." *Discover Tartini, tARTini-Turismo culturale all'insegna di Giuseppe Tartini (Interreg ITA–SLO)*, 2019–2020. http://catalog.discovertartini.eu/dcm/gt/navigation.xq

Discography

Tartini, Giuseppe. *Cantabile e suonabile.* Duo Tartini: David Plantier, Annabelle Luis. AgOgique, CD AGO020. 2015.

Tartini, Giuseppe. *Continuo addio!* Duo Tartini: David Plantier, Annabelle Luis. Muso CD MU- 031. 2019.

Tartini, Giuseppe. *Senti lo mare. Sonates pour violon seul.* Matthieu Camilleri. En Phases, CD ENP002. 2018.

Tartini, Giuseppe. *Tartini: Violin Concertos.* Chouchane Siranossian, Venice Baroque Orchestra, Andrea Marcon. Alpha CD ALPHA596. 2020.

Tartini, Giuseppe. *The Violin concertos (Complete) (box set).* L'arte dell'arco. Dynamic CDS7713. 2015.

Tartini, Giuseppe. *Vertigo (The Last Violin Sonatas).* Duo Tartini: David Plantier, Annabelle Luis. Muso CD MU- 040. 2020.

The Production of Sound: Instruments
and Bows in Tartini's Time

Donatella Melini

String Instrument Bows in the Arts at the Time of Tartini

Abstract: At the time Giuseppe Tartini lived, the bows of string instruments were in full evolution. In accordance with the repertoire, but also with geographic tradition, bows could vary in length as well as the shape of the tips and horsehair attachment. In order to retrace the long path that led to the standardized bow as we know it today, the musical iconography (paintings, drawings, etc.), musical treatises (especially regarding violin techniques) and the testimony of correspondences are of fundamental importance, owing to the very small number of bows we have today dating to that era.

Keywords: Bow, iconography, organology, *archetier* tradition, violin methods

From the sixteenth century onwards, stringed instruments were subjected to extensive experimentation, as regards the most appropriate materials and construction techniques, in order to provide them with that voice and proper response that best met the needs of contemporary performance practice. Even if, in general, we tend to think of the instrument only as the result of a refined assembly of woods, we must not forget the absolute importance of research in the field of harmonic strings and bow making that over the centuries closely accompanied, then as today, the evolution of instrumental technique. How to rub the string, how to make it vibrate in the best possible way and how to highlight the musician's personality, intentions and executive needs: these are some of the basic issues to which the art of bow making has been trying to give adequate answers since ancient times. The evolution of the bow – beginning with the simple bundles of vegetable fibre tied to the end of a branch and bent in an arch introduced to the West by the Moors in the tenth century – has indeed been a long one.

Unfortunately, the very small number of surviving bows built at least until the mid-eighteenth century makes the search difficult and complicated. Despite this *impasse*, it is still possible to (1) "visualize" its evolution through the iconography; (2) outline this evolution with reference to the treatises and methods dedicated to the art of playing proficiently; (3) appreciate the results and the impact on performance practice through the descriptions of sound impressions preserved in letters and reviews.

In ancient times, the bows were mostly made with local woods, usually of fruit trees, as they are very uniform and compact, and above all cheap and easy to find. Already in the tenth century, horsehair was preferred to vegetable fibre. It was tied to the ends of the bow (sometimes passing through a hole) and held in tension by the fingers of the right hand. The iconography, in this regard, provides several interesting examples, although it often does not properly represent the length of the bows in relation to the size of the depicted instrument; as is well known, iconography must always be "interpreted" and is almost never the objective mirror of the reality it reflects.[1] This type of bow, with minor innovations, is still in use today in various folk contexts all over the world. From the end of the fourteenth century, the manufacturing of the bow began a development that around the middle of the fifteenth century led to the acquisition of a block of wood, the ancestor of the frog, which facilitated, though still in a rudimentary way, the grip on the right hand for tightening the horsehair.

In the sixteenth century, a season of great transformations for the bowed string instruments began. This development is also attested in treatises,[2] which were enriched by increasingly detailed illustrations and also compiled to reflect on different origins and types, uses and repertoires (Fig. 1). The constructive evolution of the viola da gamba and the violin family also gave rise to great experimentation, prompting the construction of a bow increasingly suited to the new instrumental needs. In fact, the bow began to acquire particular shapes in order to better support the musicians's movements and the tensions produced by rubbing the hairs on the strings. In this perspective, the choice of wood became more and more meticulous, with a preference for exotic essences (above all "snakewood")[3] over the common essences of fruit trees. In the first decades of the seventeenth century, iconography provides evidence of different types of bows. For example, we can see bows with a bunch of horsehairs fixed to the top of the stick (Fig. 2) with the aid of a cap (of ivory or wood) and, at the opposite end, a fixed frog in which the fingers stretch them. We also find other kinds of bow whose hairs are fixed at the tip inside an *ad hoc* hole (the "mortise") and anchored in the same way to the heel after passing over its outer edge; this can also be seen in plate XXI of the *Theatrum instrumentorum seu Sciagraphia* by Michael Praetorius[4] (Fig. 3).

---

1   See Donatella Melini, *Nella bottega del liutaio – storia e tecnologia degli strumenti a pizzico e ad arco* (Lucca: Libreria Musicale Italiana, 2021), 17–21.

2   Among the first: Sebastian Virdung, *Musica getutsch und außgezogen* (Basel, 1511); Martin Agricola, *Musica instrumentalis deudsch* (Wittemberg, 1529).

3   *Brosimum guianense* is a hard and compact wood. It is commonly called snakewood because of its particular colouring.

4   Michael Praetorius, *Syntagmatis Musici* (Brunswick, 1615–19). The three-volume treatise is to be considered the first real modern treatise on organology which, not surprisingly, takes its name from it. The first volume is entitled, *De Musica Sacra* (1615); the second, *De Organographia* (1619), speaks of musical instruments and the third, without a specific title (1619), describes musical forms. In 1620, the second volume was enriched with a graphic appendix entitled *Theatrum instrumentorum*

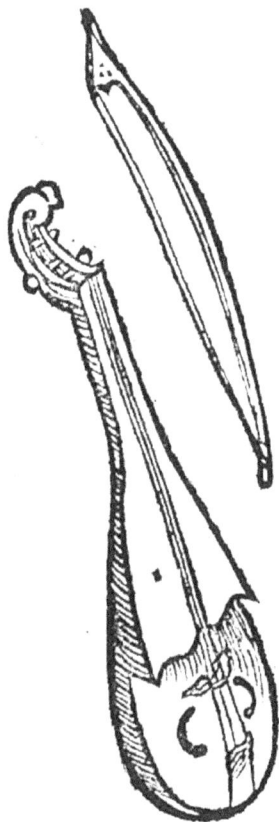

Fig. 1: Rebec and bow from Martin Agricola. Musica instrumentalis deudsch,
1528, f. 55v

seu Sciagraphia in which 42 accurate woodcuts group the instruments mainly into
families (or into ensembles or instruments of the same era).

Fig. 2: Judith Leyster, Young flute player, 1630. Nationalmuseum, Stockholm

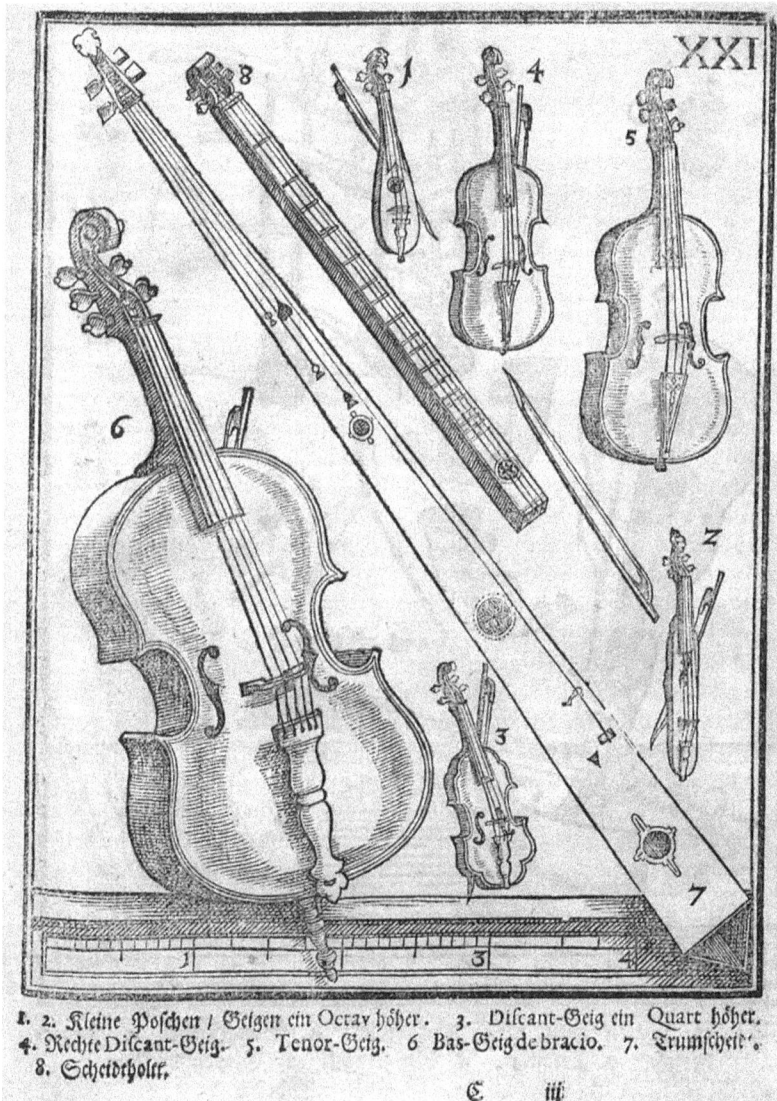

Fig. 3: Plate XXI from Michael Praetorius. Sciagraphia, 1620

In the second half of the century, the frog acquired an increasingly important role: it became mobile and equipped with a sort of hook or ring (called a
crémaillère) to hold it in position. It was fixed on notches made in the final part
of the stick. The stick was sometimes finished with a kind of button, often made
of ivory, which, at least initially, was only an ornament. Only in the last years of
the seventeenth century did this button, perhaps to solve the difficulty of the rack,
acquire the function that we still recognize today: that of stretching the horsehair with the aid of the screw connected to it. With the aid of a ring, it allows the
frog to slide at the end of the stick. With their desire for new timbres and their
constantly evolving performing needs, instrumentalists asked the bowmakers to
produce a bow with a grip and hold that was satisfactory along its whole length.
They wished to maintain the same strength of sound in all its parts, and they also
wanted the bow to respond brilliantly to the increasingly complex bow strokes at
both the heel and head and to make the changes in accents, climaxes, crescendos
and strengths more fluid. To meet these needs, the builders began to focus on the
shape of the bow, in particular the stick and its head, developing over the course of
time two main types: the "pike" and the "swan-neck". The pike-head model takes
its bizarre name from the shape of the low and slender tip, which reminded one
of the characteristic profiles of this freshwater fish's snout. The angle at the tip
between the hair and the stick is acute; the stick, with a round or oval section, is
almost straight when at rest, while it curves outwards when under tension; and the
frog, which is wedged into a special space carved into the wood of the stick, could
be adjusted, thanks to that rack mentioned above, only partially and almost never
while playing. However, owing to the shape of the head and to the narrow angle
between the hair and the stick, the pike-head bow had a limited and weak sound
towards the tip and for this reason was unsuited to repertoires that required much
more pronounced sonorities. To overcome this problem, the space between the
horsehair and the stick was greatly increased at the tip. Thus, a new type of bow
was born called (because of its particular shape) "swan-necked". The horsehairs are
placed directly in the frog which, thanks to the button now equipped with a screw,
can stretch or loosen them. On the function of the frog, the iconography offers
several curious examples in portraits of musicians playing instruments of the *viola
da braccio* family. In these paintings, the instrumentalist's right hand is often not
placed on the frog but further on towards the centre of the stick.[5] It must be said,
obviously, that there is no clear line of demarcation (geographical or temporal)
between the use and/or abandonment of the specific types of bow. In this case,
the iconography does not help to give precise and unambiguous answers. And

---

5   For example: *The Violin Player* painted by Gerard van Honthorst in 1626, today
    preserved at the Mauritshuis of Hague, or the *Portrait of Luigi Boccherini* painted
    probably by Pompeo Batoni around 1764, today preserved at the National Gallery
    of Victoria in Melbourne.

generally speaking, even the connection between a particular model of bow and a geographically characterized repertoire is a topic that is hardly clear (if at all).

An example is provided by Abbot François Raguenet in his *Parallèle des Italiens et des François en ce qui regarde la musique et les opéra*, published in Paris.[6] From 1697 to 1698, Raguenet made a long journey to Italy in the *entourage* of Cardinal de Bouillon and wrote his own impressions of Italian music by comparing it with the French. Violins, bows, their use and sound in performance are the subjects of interesting observation:

> As for the instruments, our violins are superior to those of Italy for finesse and deli-cacy of play. All the bowings of the Italians are very hard as they are detached from each other; and when they want to bind them, they move the bow in a very disagree-able way. (p. 17)

> They [the Italians] imprint the character so well in their Airs, that reality often does not act more strongly on the soul; everything there is so lively, so acute, so piercing, so impetuous and so stirring, that the imagination, the senses, the soul, and the body itself are carried away by a common transport; one cannot refrain from following the rapidity of these movements; a symphony of Furies agitates the soul, upsets it, topples it in spite of itself; the violin player who performs it cannot help being transported by it and taking the fury of it, he torments his violin, his body, he is no longer master of himself, he is agitated like one possessed, he could not do otherwise. If the Symphony is to express calm and repose, although it demands an entirely opposite character, they execute it no less successfully; these are notes which descend so low that they sink the soul with them in their depth; they are bow strokes of infinite length, trailing with a dying sound that grows ever weaker until it expires entirely. I have never heard anything, in terms of Symphonies, comparable to that which was performed in Rome, at the Oratoire de S. Jérôme de la Charité (Oratorio di San Girolamo della Carità), on Saint Martin's Day in the year 1697, on these two words, *mille saette*, a thousand arrows: it was an Air whose Notes were dotted in the manner of Gigues; the char-acter of this Air imprinted so vividly on the soul the idea of an arrow; and the force of this idea so seduced the imagination, that each violin seemed to be a bow, and all the Bows, so many shot arrows whose points seemed to transfix the Symphony from all sides; one could not hear anything more ingenious and more felicitously expressed. All this, whether the Airs are of a lively character or of a tender character, or whether they are impetuous. (pp. 43–48)

> The Italians still have, for the Instruments and for those who touch them, the same advantage that they have over us, for the voices and for the people who sing. Their violins have thicker strings than ours, they have much longer bows, and they know how to draw more sound from their instruments than we do. For me, the first time that I heard the Orchestra of our Opera on my return from Italy, the idea of the strength

---

6   François Raguenet, *Parallèle des Italiens et des François en ce qui regarde la musique et les opéra* (Paris: Jean Moreau, 1702).

of these sounds which was still present to me, made me find our violins so weak that
I thought they all had mutes. (pp. 103–104)[7]

Despite the first impression, which was certainly not flattering, Raguenet admits
that the bows of the Italians, thanks to their greater length, were able to sustain
coups d'archet d'une longueur infinie giving rise to a more consistent and evidently
very engaging sound.

The few pike-head bows that have come to us generally have a length between
58.4 and 64 cm while that of the swan-necked bows is around 70 cm. These
dimensions and the succession from one bow model to the other were not a rigid
rule, and there are illustrious exceptions. Indeed, it is interesting to reflect on the

---

7 François Raguenet, *Parallèle:* Quant aux instruments, nos violons sont au-dessus
   de ceux d'Italie pour la finesse e la délicatesse du jeu. Tous les coups d'archet des
   Italiens sont très durs lors qu'ils sont détachez les uns des autres; et lors qu'ils les
   veulent lier, ils viellent d'une manière très désagréable. (p. 17)
      Ils [les italiens] en impriment si bien le caractère dans leurs Airs, que souvent
   la réalité n'agit pas plus fortement sur l'âme; tout y est si vif, si aigu, si perçant, si
   impétueux et si remuant, que l'imagination, les sens, l'âme, et le corps même en
   sont entraînez d'un commun transport; on ne peut se défendre de suivre la rapidité
   de ces mouvements; une symphonie de Furies agite l'âme, la renverse, la culbute
   malgré elle; le Joueur de violon qui l'exécute ne peut s'empêcher d'en être transporté
   et d'en prendre la fureur, il tourmente son violon, son corps, il n'est plus maître de
   lui-même, il s'agite comme un possédé, il ne saurait faire autrement. Si la Symphonie
   doit exprimer le calme et le repos, quoi qu'elle demande un caractère tout opposé,
   ils ne l'exécutent pas avec moins de succès; ce sont des tons qui descendent si bas,
   qu'ils abîment l'âme avec eux dans leur profondeur; ce sont des coups d'archet
   d'une longueur infinie, traînez d'un son mourant qui s'affaiblit toujours jusqu'à ce
   qu'il expire entièrement. Je n'ay jamais rien entendu, en matière de Symphonies, de
   comparable à celle qui fut exécutée à Rome, à l'Oratoire de S. Jérôme de la Charité,
   le jour de la Saint Martin de l'année 1697, sur ces deux mots, *mille saette*, mille
   flèches: c'était un Air dont les Notes étaient pointées à la manière des Gigues; le
   caractère de cet Air imprimait si vivement dans l'âme l'idée de flèche; et la force de
   cette idée séduisait tellement l'imagination, que chaque violon paraissait être un arc,
   et tous les Archets, autant de flèches décochées dont les pointes semblaient darder la
   Symphonie de toutes parts; on ne saurait entendre rien de plus ingénieux et de plus
   heureureusement [sic] exprimé. Ainsi, soit que les Airs soient d'un caractère vif ou
   d'un caractère tendre, soit qu'ils soient impétueux (pp. 43–48).
      Les Italiens ont encore, pour les Instruments et pour ceux qui les touchent, le
   même avantage qu'ils ont sur nous, pour les voix et pour les personnes qui chantent.
   Leurs violons sont montez de cordes plus grosses que les nôtres, ils ont des archets
   beaucoup plus longs, et ils savent tirer de leurs Instruments une fois plus de son,
   que nous. Pour moi, la première fois que j'entendis l'Orchestre de notre Opéra à
   mon retour d'Italie, l'idée de la force de ces sons qui m'était encore présente, me fit
   trouver ceux de nos violons si faibles, que je crus qu'ils avoient tous des sourdines.
   (pp. 103–4)

experimental scope of the eighteenth century. It was a century during which a type of wood originating from Brazil began to be preferred, namely *pernambuco* and during which a model of bow was created – it was later given the name "classical" or "transitional"[8] – which subsequently, thanks to the great tradition of French bowmakers, opened the way to the modern bow.

One illustrious exception is given by the two bows of Giuseppe Tartini (Fig. 4) preserved at the Giuseppe Tartini Conservatory in Trieste. Although both have a length of 71.3 cm, one belongs to the pike-head model (no. 1), the other to the swan-necked type (no. 2). In this regard, Antonino Airenti observes:

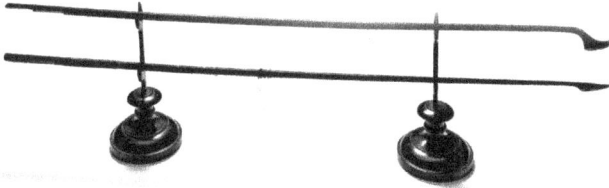

Fig. 4: Tartini's bows. Conservatorio di musica, Trieste

Tartini's second bow has many of the characteristics of a classical bow but still has a clip-in frog. In a complete state this bow in serviceable condition should weigh about 44.4 grams (stick 34.9g; frog 7g; horsehair 2.5g), whilst to have the same mechanical properties, a bow with screw should weigh around 50g (the screw, nut and endpin together weigh about 5.5g) which would be quite a common weight classical violin bow. Experience, corroborated by scientific research, shows that the tension screw mechanism deprives the bow of the possibility of being able to emit several important harmonics. We may therefore assume that Tartini's classical bow was more agile (because of being less heavy) and able to emit a more complete timbre (lacking a screw) than other classical bows of the times. An anonymous painting portrays the elderly Tartini[9] with a bow very similar to this one. This unique bow raises interesting questions to which we do not know the answers: is its form the result of Tartini's

---

8   The terms are in fact equivalent; "classical" is used in relation to the music of the classical period, "transitional" in relation to the transition from the baroque to the modern bow.

9   See *infra.*

endless research and experimentation, or does it represent the desire of a man, already getting on in years, not to cut himself off completely from a baroque style which was by then in the past? [10]

Fig. 5: Tartini's portrait. Conservatorio di musica, Trieste

---

10 Paolo Da Col, Airenti Antonino and Federico Lowenberger, "The Tartini Violin Relics", *The Galpin Society Journal* 64 (2011): 248–61: 257.

Airenti cites a portrait of Tartini (Fig. 5) which is today part of the so-called *cimeli tartiniani* (Tartini relics) preserved at the Conservatorio di Trieste. In my opinion,[11] it is the archetype for both the most famous engraving made by Carlo Calcinotto in Padua in 1763 and the portrait requested by Father Martini for his own picture gallery.[12] In addition, this portrait shows a bow clearly endowed with a considerable distance between the head and the horsehair, though the length of the stick is apparently more contained. The importance of the bow in Tartini's work is well known and has been widely studied, but it is interesting, in my opinion, to reread at least two letters from his correspondence also from a more strictly "constructive" point of view. What transpires is how much the bow – and the research (in full ferment in those years) regarding the most suitable shape and materials – influenced and codified the famous Tartini "sound":

Gian Rinaldo Carli to Tartini – From Venice, 21 August 1743

[...] To the depth of your meditations, the merit of so much beauty and of so many phenomena discovered in music is due; among which phenomena, I will always recount the one which you explained to me with so much wisdom and readiness, when two years ago I entreated you to tell me the reason why the more one presses the bow against the strings, the less the sound is heard from a certain distance; whereas from nearby it becomes noisy and more harsh and unpleasant than usual. You told me then that when the bow is drawn with dexterity horizontally over the string, a horizontal and distinct oscillation occurs, which, impressing on the air an undulation which is successive and precise, makes it so that the sound carries to the greatest possible distance. But if, on the contrary, one presses the string perpendicularly when bowing, two different oscillations are born thereof, one perpendicular, the other horizontal; therefore mixing with one another, and mutually destroying one another, the undulation of the air is no longer simple and direct, but swirling and uncertain; and therefore just as the sound can only be harsh and noisy from nearby, for the same reason it cannot extend itself, as in the first case, to an equal distance. I then realised why your violin distinguishes itself above all other violins, and why your bowing sounds so pleasant and so delicate. [...][13]

11 Melini Donatella, "Una maschera, un ritratto, un nome: Giuseppe Tartini e i cimeli del conservatorio di Trieste all'origine dell'iconografia tartiniana," *Liuteria Musica Cultura*, 2 (2016): 48–54.
12 Painting by an anonymous seventeenth-century Venetian painter, Museo internazionale e biblioteca della musica di Bologna, inv. B 11879 /B 39205.
13 Giuseppe Tartini, *Lettere e documenti*, ed. Giorgia Malagò, vol. II (Trieste: EUT, Edizioni Università di Trieste, 2020), 295–96. For the Italian text, see vol. I, p. 156: Alla intensione delle vostre meditazioni è dovuto il merito di tante bellezze, e di tanti fenomeni scoperti nella musica; frai quali io conterò sempre quello, che con tanta sagacità, e prontezza mi avete spiegato, allorché due anni sono vi pregai di dirmi la ragione perché quanto più si preme l'arco sulle corde, tanto meno il suono si sente ad una data distanza, nel mentre che da vicino diviene strepitoso, e più del solito aspro

Tartini to Maddalena Lombardini-Sirmen – Padua, 5 March, 1760.

At last, by the will of God, I have found myself freed of the weighty business which
has so long prevented me from keeping my promise to you, a promise which was
made with too much sincerity for my lack of time not to afflict me. Let us begin, in
God's name, by letter; and if you should not understand what I write here, I entreat
you to write and ask me to explain all that you do not understand. Your principal practice and study should be confined in general to the bow, in order to entirely master
whatever can be played or sung. Your first study, therefore, should be holding, bal-
ancing and pressing the bow lightly in such a manner that it shall seem to breathe the
first note and not to strike the string. This depends on lightness of wrist, and if you
make the bow move immediately after laying the bow lightly on the strings there is no
longer any danger of roughness or harshness. You should master this first, very light,
contact in every part of the bow, in the middle as well as at the extremities; and you
must master both the upbow and downbow [...].[14]

From these letters, it is clear how important it was both that the horsehair should
adhere strongly to the strings in all parts of the bow and that the bow should
be adequately moved horizontally, seeking a good balance between strength and
movement of the wrist. These skills were made possible, thanks to all the research

---

ed ingrato. Mi diceste allora, che stirando l'arco con destrezza orizzontalmente sulla
corda, ne succede un'oscillazione orizzontale e distinta, la quale imprimendo nell'aria
un'ondulazione successiva e precisa, fa che il suono pervenga alla maggiore distanza
possibile. Ma se all'opposto stirando l'arco si preme perpendicolarmente la corda,
due diverse oscillazioni ne nascono, una perpendicolare, e l'altra orizzontale; onde
una con l'altra confondendosi, e mutualmente distruggendosi, l'onda dell'aria non
è più semplice e diretta, ma vorticosa e incerta; e però come da vicino il suono non
può essere se non che aspro e rumoroso, così non può estendersi, come nel primo
caso, ad un'eguale distanza. Conobbi allora perché il vostro violino si distingua sopra
tutti gli altri violini, e perché il suono della vostra arcata riesca così aggradevole, e
così delicato.

14 Tartini, *Lettere e documenti*, vol. II, p. 426. The Italian text is in vol. I, p. 228: Signora
    Madalena mia stimatissima, finalmente quando a Dio è piaciuto mi sono sbrigato da
    quella grave occupazione, che fin qui mi ha impedito di mantenerle la mia promessa,
    sebben anche troppo mi stava al cuore, perché di fatto m'afligeva la mancanza di
    tempo. Incominciamo adunque col nome di Dio per lettera, e se quanto qui espongo
    ella non intende abbastanza, mi scriva, e dimandi spiegazione di tutto ciò, che non
    intende. Il di lei esercizio, e studio principale deve esser l'arco in genere, cosiché
    ella se ne faccia padrona assoluta a qualunque uso o suonabile, o cantabile. Primo
    studio deve esser l'appoggio dell'arco sulla corda siffattamente leggiero, che il primo
    principio della voce, che si cava sia come un fiatto [sic], e non come una percossa
    sulla corda. Consiste in leggierezza di polso, e in prosseguir subito l'arcata, doppo
    l'appoggio legiero non v'è più pericolo d'asprezza, e crudezza. Di questo appoggio,
    così leggiero ella deve farsi padrona in qualunque sitto [sic] dell'arco, sia in mezzo,
    sia negli estremi, e deve esserne padrona coll'arcata in su, e coll'arcata in giù.

and experiments carried out in the same years – in particular on the correct ribbon distribution of the hairs, on the search for adequate elasticity and strength of the stick (thanks to the use of pernambuco), and on the study of its curvature through different forms of diameter and sections. The great experimenters in this field were above all the French: in particular the Tourte family, acknowledged as the founders of the great French *archetier* tradition, whose members collaborated with violinists such as Wilhelm Cramer and Giovanni Battista Viotti.[15]

Tartini was certainly not the only one to reflect on the importance of the bow and to recommend its correct use in his teaching prescriptions. Francesco Geminiani published in Paris an enlarged edition accompanied by tables of his method, *The Art of Playing on the Violin*, published in London in 1751.[16] *L'art du Violon ou Méthode Raisonnée* devotes a significant part to the bow (how to hold it and how to use it):

> The quality of the sound you can get from the violin absolutely depends on how carefully the bow is handled. The elasticity of the wrist, and the more or less heaviness, force, and balance produce these delicate, pleasant, speaking, sometimes delightful sounds that can be drawn from this instrument.[17]

Leopold Mozart in his famous *Versuch einer gründlichen Violinschule* (Augsburg 1756 followed by various revisions, extensions and translations) dedicated a section, chapter VII, to the "Many Varieties of Bowing" (*Von den vielen Veränderungen des Bogenstrichs*). At the beginning of this section, it is interesting to read about the sonic (and also emotional) effects that can result from a good use of the bow:

> The present chapter will convince us entirely that the bowing gives life to the notes; that it produces now a modest, now an impertinent, now a serious or playful tone; now coaxing, or grave and subline; now a sad or merry melody; and is therefore the medium by the reasonable use of which we are able to rouse in the hearers the aforesaid affects.[18]

---

15 Nicolas Léonard Tourte, called *l'aîné*, collaborated with Cramer in the study of the shapes of the head. His brother François Xavier Tourte, called *le jeune*, with the help of Viotti developed a new type of flattened frog that improved how the bundle of hair was spread through a wedge, a metal ring placed at the attachment of the frog, and the insertion of a mother-of-pearl slide to close the passage of the horsehair.

16 Francesco Geminiani, *The Art of Playing on the Violin*, op. IX (London: 1751).

17 Francesco Geminiani, *L'art du violon ou Méthode raisonnée* (Paris: Sibert, n.d.), 5: La qualité du son qu'on tire du violon dépend absolutement du ménagement de l'Archet. L'élasticité du poignet, et le plus ou moins de pésanteur, de force, et d'equilibre produisent ces sons délicates, agréables, parlantes, quelque fois ravissantes, qu'on peut tirer de cet instrument.

18 Leopold Mozart, *Treatise on the Fundamentals of Violin Playing*, trans. Editha Knocker (Oxford: University Press, 1948), 114.

In paragraph 17, we read considerations on the weight of the bow and practical instructions on how to behave depending on the length of the bow:

> The weight of a violin bow contributes much, as does also in no less degree its length or shortness. A heavier and longer bow must be used more lightly and retarded somewhat less; whereas a lighter and shorter bow must be pressed down more and retarded more. Above all, the right hand must here be made a little stiff, but the contracting and relaxing of the same must be regulated according to the weight and length, or the lightness and shortness of the bow.[19]

The new frontiers of performance that were developed in the last decades of the eighteenth century coincided, therefore, with the sublime art of bowing to which musicians, teachers and composers paid increasing attention. Even the history of the evolution of the bow began to arouse interest and to occupy a position of importance in the practical instruction books. This is demonstrated by the violinist Michel Woldemar, who in his *Grande méthode* inserts a table that summarizes this history, also accompanying it with illustrations (Fig. 6) that will later be repeated many times by other authors. Woldemar writes:

> The four different bows are those ones which have been successively in use since the origin of the violin.
>
> no. 1 shows that of Corelli, very arched. Short and pointed, it derives from that of the Bass Viola, an instrument prior to the violin.
>
> no. 2, the bow of Tartini, successor of Corelli, his master; it is longer and higher at the head.
>
> no. 3 is that of Cramer of Mannheim; it was adopted in its time by the majority of the artists and amateurs.
>
> no. 4 comes to us from the famous Viotti; it differs little from that of Cramer at the head, but the frog is lower and closer to the button; it is longer and has more horsehair; it is played a little relaxed and is today almost alone in use.[20]

---

19 Leopold Mozart, *Treatise*, 119.
20 Woldemar Michel, *Grande méthode, ou, étude élémentaire pour le violon, contenant un grand nombre de gammes, toutes les positions du violon, et leur doigter ; tous les coups d'archet anciens et nouveaux l'echelle enharmonique moderne fugues, des exemples d'après les plus grands maitres* (Paris: Hanry, 1800?), 4: Les quatre différents Archets sont ceux qui ont été successivement en usage depuis l'origin du violon. /Le n.1 représente celui de Corelli très arqué. Courte et pointu, il dérive celui de la Basse de Viole, instrument anterieur au violon. /Le n.2, l'archet de Tartini successeur de Corelli, son maitre, il est plus long et plus elevé de tête. /Le n.3, est celui de Cramer de Manheim, il fut adopté dans son temps, par la majorité des Artistes et des Amateur. /Le n.4 nous vient du célèbre Viotti, il diffère peu de celui de Cramer pour la tête, mais la hausse est plus base et plus rapprochée du bouton, il est plus long et porte plus de crin, il se joue un peu détendu et est aujourd'hui presque seul en usage.

Les quatre différents Archets sont ceux qui ont été successivement en usage depuis l'origine du Violon.

Le N°. 1 représente celui de Corelli très arqué, court et pointu. il dérive de celui de la Basse de Viole, instrument antérieur au Violon.

Le N°. 2, l'Archet de Tartini successeur de Corelli son maître. il est plus long et plus élevé de tête.

Le N°. 3 est celui de Cramer de Manheim, il fut adopté dans son tems, par la majorité des Artistes et des Amateurs.

Le N°. 4 nous vient du célèbre Viotti, il diffère peu de celui de Cramer pour la tête, mais la hausse est plus basse et plus raprochée du bouton, il est plus long et porte plus de crin; il se joue un peu détendu et est aujourd'hui presque seul en usage.

N°. 1. Archet de Corelli.

N°. 2. Archet de Tartini.

N°. 3. Archet de Cramer.

N°. 4. Archet de Viotti.

TOUCHE représentant touttes les positions du violon prises au 1er. doigt jusqu'au sib. passé lequel il n'y a plus de position entiere et l'on doigte selon les chiffres en observant que le dernier Si doit être harmonique.

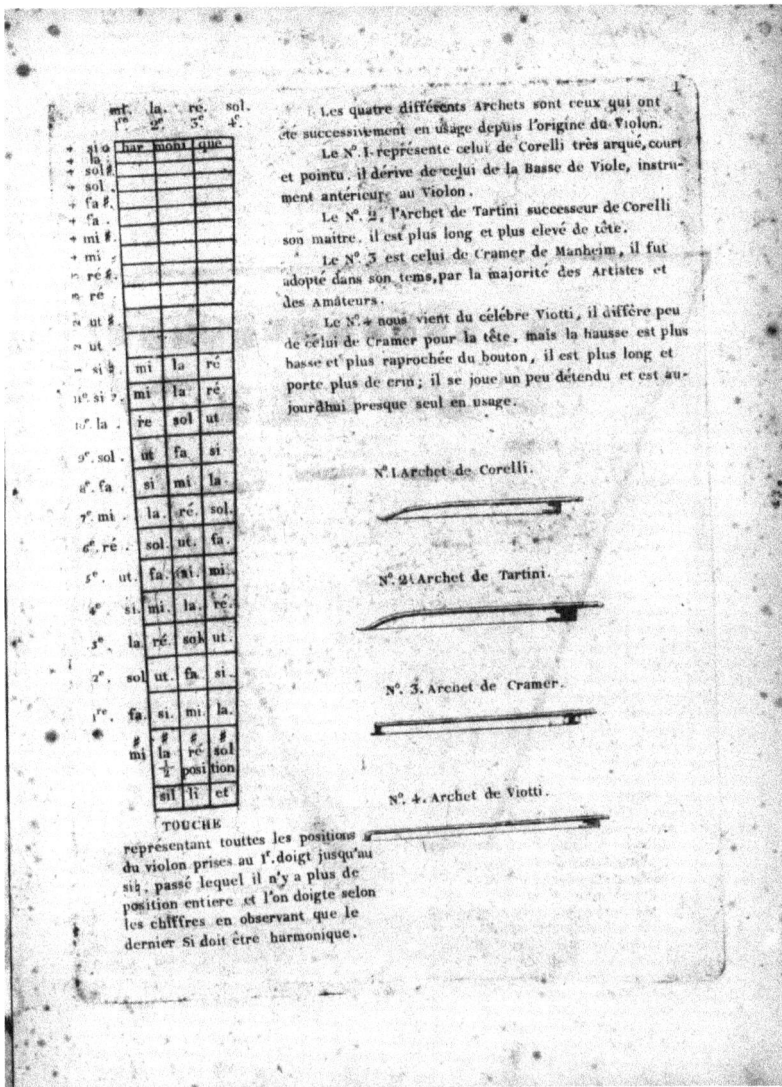

Fig. 6: Woldemar, table with the evolution of the bow

Bibliography

Da Col, Paolo, Antonino Airenti and Federico Lowenberger. "The Tartini Violin Relics." *The Galpin Society Journal* 64 (2011): 248–61, 198–99.

Geminiani, Francesco. *L'Art du Violon ou Méthode Raisonnée pour aprendre a bien jouer de cet Instrument. Composéee primitivement par le Célébre F. Geminiani, et nouvellement Redigée, Augmentée, Expliquée et enrichie de nouveaux exempler, Préludes, Airs et Duos gradués pour éclaircir et faciliter l'instruction et mettre évidement en pratique les principes de cet excellent maitre. Nouvelle édition. Mise au jour d'apres les Conseils, les Soins, les Exemples et les productions des plus habiles maitres de Violon, Francais, Italiens et Allemans.* Paris: chez Sibert, n.d.

Melini, Donatella. "Una maschera, un ritratto, un nome: Giuseppe Tartini e i cimeli del Conservatorio di Trieste all'origine dell'iconografia tartiniana." *Liuteria Musica Cultura* 2 (2016): 48–54.

Melini, Donatella. *Nella bottega del liutaio – storia e tecnologia degli strumenti a pizzico e ad arco.* Lucca: Libreria Musicale Italiana, 2021.

Mozart, Leopold. *Treatise on the Fundamentals of Violin Playing.* Translated by Editha Knocker. Oxford: University Press, 1948.

Raguenet, François. *Parallèle des Italiens et des François en ce qui regarde la musique et les opéra.* Paris: chez Jean Moreau, 1702.

Tartini, Giuseppe. *Lettere e documenti.* Edited by Giorgia Malagò, vols. I, II. Trieste: EUT, Edizioni Università di Trieste, 2020.

Woldemar Michel. *Grande méthode, ou, étude élémentaire pour le violon, contenant un grand nombre de gammes, toutes les positions du violon, et leur doigter; tous les coups d'archet anciens et nouveaux l'echelle enharmonique moderne fugues, des exemples d'après les plus grands maitres … Paris: Cochet, [1798].*

Johannes Loescher

Violin Making during Tartini's Working Life

Abstract: This chapter highlights Giuseppe Tartini's contribution to Italian violin making. Tartini's involvement with violin playing and technique over decades was accompanied by his intense pursuit of technical improvement in violin making. Some of his violin innovations, such as the use of thicker gut strings, the modified shape of the violin bow stick and a bridge design that created changes in sound quality, can be traced back to Tartini himself. As regards their construction, mention should be made of violin makers mainly from Venice, but in particular, Antonio Bagatella, who worked in Padua, and was closely associated with Tartini for many years. In addition, as a violinist, Tartini seems to have been a connoisseur and expert in antique instruments, with which he most probably traded as well.

Keywords: Violin making, Tartini Relics, Antonio Bagatella, Antonio Stradivari

The State of Italian Violin Making in the Second Third of the Eighteenth Century

During Giuseppe Tartini's relatively long life, several modifications and revisions took place in Italian violin making. When Tartini's musical activity began in Padua, classical violin making in Cremona had already reached its peak and, following the death of Antonio Stradivari in 1737, it finally lost its paramount importance. This does not mean, of course, that the instruments made there were no longer appreciated, but that the violin makers who continued their business there no longer exerted the formative and innovative influence that had cemented Cremona's supremacy for almost 200 years from its beginnings with Andrea Amati. By then, Venice, Milan and Naples had become important centres of supra-regional significance. Because of their historical importance as bustling trading centres, the latter cities probably also brought a new spirit to violin making. The nobility and the church ceased to be so important as the customers; production was geared to broader sales domestically and abroad, and presumably, there was a quicker response to changing musical needs and tastes. This may also explain why the restoration of some older violins began at an early age in the course of the second third of the eighteenth century. Above all, the replacement of the bridge and the fingerboard, which was usually made of lighter wood, with solid ebony seems to have been a common practice, which reportedly went back as far as the 1730s.[1]

---

1   Christian Ahrens and Bernhard Hentrich, "'Von einer steiner Violino daß grifbreth erhöhet...'. Tiefgreifende Reparaturen an Cremoneser und Stainer'schen Violinen in den 1730er-und 1740er-Jahren," in *Unisonus. Musikinstrumente erforschen, bewahren,*

The augmented height of the fingerboard, referred to on several occasions, points to a corresponding change in the height of the bridge. This seems to have reached its highest point at the end of the century, when bridges could be found up to 1 cm higher than their baroque counterparts, which means over 30 % higher than baroque bridges!

The Violin Bridge from Tartini's Artefacts

The importance of the possessions from Tartini's estate is determined by their quality, on the one hand, and by their extraordinarily detailed documented and attested origin, on the other.[2] Tartini's bows were indeed acknowledged as substantial proof of the changes to bow making.[3] At this point, I would like to attempt to classify the surviving violin bridge. The dating of bridges is usually a very laborious task. Even if signed and therefore attributable to a specific maker, or at any rate their workshop, there is usually a time span ranging from several years to decades for their possible construction.[4] In the absence of any form of signature, only stylistic comparisons can be used to attempt a rough estimate of the time of origin. Unfortunately, there are virtually no surviving originals or designs of violin bridges from the second third of the eighteenth century, which is why the one in Tartini's possession is so important. An allegedly contemporary bridge from that period can be seen in the portrait of Gaetano Pugnani with his violin, although it does not show any specific similarity in its design; in fact, it seems rather more conservative in its conception, especially because of its robust bridge feet:

sammeln, ed. Beatrix Darmstädter and Ina Hoheisel (Vienna: Praesens, 2014), 240–55, and Giuliana Montanari, "Conservazione e restauro degli strumenti ad arco alla corte di Firenze in epoca lorenese (1730–70)," *Liuteria, Musica e Cultura*, ed. Renato Meucci (1997), 3–19.

2   Paolo Da Col, Antonino Airenti and Federico Lowenberger, "The Tartini Violin Relics," *The Galpin Society Journal* 64 (2011): 248–61.

3   In this respect, see the well-known illustration, "N° 6. -Tartini, 1740." of the bows illustrated in François-Joseph Fétis, *Antoine Stradivari, Luthier Célèbre sous le Nom de Stradivarius* (Paris: Vuillaume 1856), 117.

4   An exception is the drawing of a bridge with the inventory number MS 143 from Antonio Stradivari's workshop, which bears the inscription "Adì Primo Agosto 1711// mostra". Figure and description in Fausto Cacciatori, *Antonio Stradivari. Disegni, modelli, forme* (Cremona: Museo del Violino, 2016), 131.

Fig. 1: Unknown painter: Gaetano Pugnani (Detail), London: Royal College of Music, after 1755

These are probably a consistent design feature of the bridges from Stradivari's workshop; as an example, the original bridge of the Medicea tenor viola from 1690 is illustrated here:

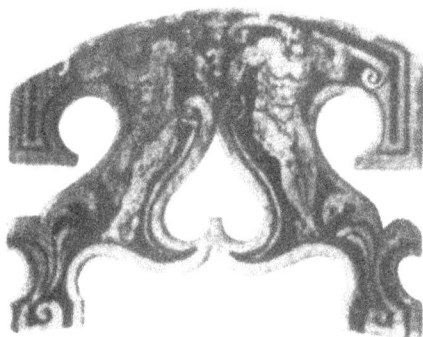

Fig. 2: Antonio Stradivari: Bridge for "Medicea" tenor viola, Florence: Galleria dell'Accademia

It is not only in the intricate workmanship of the bridge feet that the example from Tartini's estate differs from its baroque predecessors; another acoustically important change lies in the design and positioning of the two large cut-out sections towards the upper middle part on either side of the bridge:

Fig. 3: Anonymous bridge from Tartini's estate, Trieste: Conservatorio di Musica "G. Tartini".

Its shape and size, which seem unusual at first glance, allow a balanced distribution of mass and, above all, the slimming of the waist, which measures only 14.7 mm at its narrowest point. By contrast, this distance is 18 mm or more in designs of comparable size by Stradivari (MS 146 and MS 144).[5] The reduction of this distance causes a physical reduction of the stiffness; the lateral ability to vibrate around its own centre axis is thereby increased. In addition to the effects on volume and timbre,[6] the increased elasticity changes the transient wave response in my experience. The sound is perceived as more malleable and at the same time smoother and more homogeneous throughout the whole spectrum than with a baroque bridge; the notes also respond more easily. This could well reflect Tartini's musical intention, which he expressed, among other things, in his definition of *cantabile* in the "*Regole per arrivare a saper ben suonar il Violino*". Unfortunately, however, it is impossible to say with any certainty who made the bridge, and whether its design was according to Tartini's suggestion. In any case, the narrowing of the distance between the side openings can be seen in many bridges from the latter part of the eighteenth century,[7] and therefore seems to correspond to sound quality requirements typical of the time. Yet what distinguishes them considerably from the specimen from Tartini's estate is partly their exceptional height. This is due to the tendency to tilt the neck of the violin further and further back, which, because of the more acute angle of the strings over the bridge, causes significantly greater pressure on the top. However, I believe that Tartini's bridge has

---

5   See, Cacciatori, *Stradivari. Disegni, modelli, forme*, 132.
6   Joseph Curtin, "Views on the Bridge," *The Strad*, 130, no. 1555 (November 2019): 60–67.
7   See, for example, the bridges MS 1147ff. of the Museo Stradivariano, in Fausto Cacciatori, *Stradivari. Disegni, modelli, forme* (Cremona: Fondazione del Museo del Violino Antonio Stradivari Cremona, 2016), 353–55.

not survived completely in its original form, but that the height was subsequently reduced by a few millimetres. The part above the cut-outs seems disproportionately small, which is particularly noticeable given the additional balance and intentional design, and which also led to the sinking of the treble side of the wing under the pressure of the E string. Furthermore, such a light mass in the upper part inevitably leads to a very bright to pointed sound. In view of all these aspects, I suspect that the bridge originally had a height of at least 30 mm compared with today's 27 mm. This would also have made the now unusually thick upper bridge edge somewhat thinner. With this modification, I have rebuilt the bridge model several dozen times in recent years and am convinced that it helps to achieve the ideal *galant* sound of mid-eighteenth-century music.

Tartini and Violin Making

The city of Padova, where Tartini worked intermittently between 1721 and 1770, was renowned for its tradition in lutherie, largely owing to the presence of Wendelin Tieffenbrucker, an immigrant from Füssen. Nothing comparable can be found in violin making, which was perhaps also due to the proximity of Mantua and Venice, where numerous outstanding masters had lived and worked since the late seventeenth century. Of the violin makers mentioned by Willibald Leo Freiherr von Lütgendorff, namely Pietro Bagatella, Domenico dall'Oglio, Matteo Palmerio and Giacomo Zanoli, who worked only briefly in Padova, Giuseppe Galieri, Giuseppe Centurio and Santo Calzavara, only very few instruments are known to exist, if any at all.[8] Fabio Fano[9] suspects that Tartini's violin maker before 1740 was the above-mentioned Galieri or Giovanni Danieli, who, according to Lütgendorff, initially worked alone, and later with Bagatella.[10] This must have been Antonio Bagatella, as there is no evidence of any relationship to the above-mentioned Pietro Bagatella. Only a few of his instruments have survived; he is better known to later generations as the author of the *Regole per la Costruzione de' Violini Viole Violoncelli e Violoni*, which can be considered as one of the first theoretical works on violin making and was printed in 1786 at the expense of the "Accademia di Scienze, Lettere ed Arti di Padova". In the introduction to his rules, Bagatella reports on his career and his development as a violin maker. In doing so, he mentions some important details concerning his relationship with Tartini: "The opportunity to serve the renowned Signor Tartini for some 30 years, renovating violins both for him and for his many pupils, who, sent also by princes, attended

---

8   Willibald Leo Freiherr von Lütgendorff, *Die Geigen-und Lautenmacher vom Mittelalter bis zur Gegenwart*, vol. 1 (Tutzing: Schneider, 1975), 54.

9   Fabio Fano, "Bagatella," in *Dizionario Biografico degli Italiani*, vol. 5 (1963), www.treccani.it/enciclopedia/antonio-gioseffo-bagatella_%28Dizionario-Biografico%29/, retrieved on 8 January 2022.

10 Lütgendorff, *Die Geigen-und Lautenmacher*, vol. 2: 93.

his school from all over Europe, brought me many violins by the aforementioned Amati [...]."[11]

We can therefore assume that between about 1740 and 1770, there was a continuous exchange between the two and that he prepared violins for Tartini and his pupils. In fact, "accomodare" (translated as "renovate" in this text) should be understood rather literally, in the sense that it was not necessarily just a matter of repairing damage or wear, but of changing the playability. Bagatella's "discovery" of the rules of construction included a theory of the density distribution in the wood of the top and bottom sections, which he implemented not only in the making of his new violins but also in refurbishing old instruments by reworking the thicknesses of the wood, i.e. by thinning it out. In addition, he lowered the ribs in some cases. In his opinion, this improved the sound, which he demonstrated through experiments on several violins in the spaces of the Academy: "The third is by Tonon reduced by the author of the *Memoria* to the thickness measurements following his method."[12] The instrument built by Tonon is mentioned once again in the record of an examination held before a jury: "A violin belonging to Signor Conte Michele Stratico by Tonon, adjusted and reduced according to his own technique".[13]

In order to redistribute the thicknesses, Bagatella used two methods ostensibly to produce different qualities of sound. One is described as "voce umana ossia da concerto", the other as "voce argentina ossia da orchestra"; unfortunately, a more detailed description is not available.[14] Such refurbishing seems to have been carried out on many stringed instruments:

> I adapted the thicknesses of many old violins in the manner described above [...] and I will give a few examples here, since it is impossible for me to remember all those that I reduced over 35 years. I will therefore indicate some of them, some with the human voice, some with the silver voice, as I was requested to do. Signor Giuseppe Tartini had one of these ... [*There follows a long list covering almost an entire page*]. And as for Venice, in addition to the one which His Excellency Francesco Battaglia

---

11 "L'occasione di servire per il corso di circa 30 anni il celebre Sig. Tartini accomodando i Violini sì a Lui, che a tutti i suoi numerosi scolari, che mandati anche da Principi concorrevano alla sua scuola da tutta Europa, mi fece capitare alle mani molti Violini delli suddetti Amati [...]." The English versions of Bagatella's texts are by the present article's translator. Antonio Bagatella, *Regole per la Costruzione de' Violini Viole Violoncelli e Violoni, memoria presentata all'Accademia di Scienze lettere ed arti di Padova* [1782] (Padua: Zanibon, 1916), 23.

12 "[...] il terzo è di Tonon ridotto dall'Autore della Memoria alle misure di grossezza secondo il suo metodo [...]." Bagatella, *Regole*, 7. The name Tonon is probably a dialect wording of the name Tononi.

13 "Un Violino del q: Sig. Co: Michele Stratico di Tonon aggiustato e ridotto secondo il metodo dell'Autore stesso [...]." Bagatella, *Regole*, 9.

14 Bagatella, *Regole*, 3.

possesses, Messrs Giuseppe Tartini and Antonio Nazari had a great many reduced by me.[15]

The last observation suggests that Tartini was also involved in trading in violins, whether old or newly made, as the final section of the passage clearly confirms: "Of those I constructed with the said proportions and rules he possesses two […] in addition to very many others ordered by Signor Tartini, which I do not know what places he sent them to."[16]

Based on these statements, the business relationship between Tartini and Bagatella can thus be described as a close and intensive mutual exchange. After all, Bagatella was appointed by Tartini's family as a valuer for three violins from his estate: "the three violins owned by the most kind Mr Tartini which were well-known to me".[17]

Tartini's Instruments

That Giuseppe Tartini owned three violins can also be gathered from a list of expenses in a manuscript entitled "Fatti che provano la falsità del supposto che il Tartini sia uomo danaroso" ("Facts proving the falsity of the supposition that Tartini is a man of wealth"), presumably from the year 1767: "Annual expense of strings for three violins 12 ducats".[18] The resulting total of 480 ducats, noted in the manuscript, gives a term of 40 years, which is also explicitly used as a basis for his other expenses. Their regularity suggests that these were expenses for instruments permanently belonging to him. The actual makers of these violins can only be

---

15 "Adattai nel modo surriferito le grossezze a molti Violini vecchi […] e adurrò qui alcuni in esempio, essendo impossibile ch'io mi ricordi di tutti quelli, che furono da me ridotti nel corso di 35 anni. Ne additerò dunque alquanti parte di voce umana, parte di voce argentina, come mi furono ordinati. N'ebbe uno di questi il Sig. Giuseppe Tartini […] Per Venezia poi oltre a quello che tiene S. E. Francesco Battaglia, moltissimi me ne fecero ridurre i Signori Giuseppe Tartini ed Antonio Nazari." Bagatella, *Regole*, 23.

16 "De' fabbricati poi da me colle descritte proporzioni e regole due ne possede […] oltre a moltissimi altri ordinatimi dal Sig. Tartini, e che non so in quali parti sieno stati da lui mandate." Bagatella, *Regole*, 24.

17 "li tre violini del g[entilissi]m[o]: Sig[no]r: Tartini […] essendomi à me molto noti." This is evident from a document written by Bagatella and dated 7 March 1770, which can be found in Slovenia in the regional archives of Piran, Giuseppe Tartini collection, SI-PIt ms. 15, www.internetculturale.it/jmms/iccuviewer/iccu.jsp?id= oai%3Awww.internetculturale.sbn.it%2FTeca%3A20%3ANT0000%3ANT%3AASI-PIt-001 015&mode=all&teca=MagTeca+-+ICCU, retrieved on 8 January 2022.

18 "Annua spesa di corde per tre violini duc[ati]12". Laura Malagò, *Tartini. Lettere e documenti*, vol. 1 (Trieste: EUT, 2020), 339. Translation in Laura Malagò, *Tartini. Lettere e documenti*, vol. 2, 475, 477. https://www.discovertartini.eu/epistolario/I/, retrieved on 8 January 2022.

guessed at in part. At least three of Antonio Stradivari's violins are associated with Tartini: the "Vogelweith" from 1711, the "Lipinski" from 1715 and the so-called "Tartini" from around 1720–25. There is no conclusive evidence for any of them, except in the case of the "Lipinski" violin with regard to the well-known anecdote about the Italian violinist Salvini. He is said to have been one of Tartini's pupils and allegedly received the Stradivarius violin from him. Furthermore, Tartini is said to have owned a violin made by Cremonese violin maker Andrea Guarneri in 1683, the "Santa Teresa, Tartini, Sivori". Giuseppe Tartini's birthplace in Piran (Pirano) possesses a violin which, according to Eduard Melkus,[19] was a Tyrolean instrument; today it is attributed to Nicolò Marchioni Amati and was made in Bologna between 1715 and 1725.[20] What is certain is that Giuseppe Tartini owned a violin by Antonio Bagatella until his death; the story of its transfer is described in detail in *The Tartini Violin Relics*.[21]

The assumption that Tartini owned a violin by Jacob Stainer is probably inspired by the mention of a consignment of violins to the court in Dresden in a letter to Francesco Algarotti of 6 October 1746:

> The six violins are ready and put in cases for the long journey. Among those six (all good) one is certainly by Stainer, and another one more likely to be by Stainer than by another maker. The expense (including the travel case and protection of the case) is forty-one *zecchini* in total: a little money is lacking. In such transactions, precision is impossible, at the most for what could be given for one violin or two: it cannot be given for six. Furthermore, it was a stroke of luck (as has happened in the present case) to find a batch of twelve violins which are all good, and to find it in the hands of a patron of mine, who allowed me the choice and the price I set. Therefore, I honestly maintain that the intrinsic value of the six violins amounts to much more than the price given. Hence, I have the comfort of being sure of having served Your Most Illustrious Lordship well.[22]

---

19 Eduard Melkus, *Die Violine* (Bern, Hallwag 1975), 51.

20 www.portoroz.si/en/experience/events/4194, retrieved on 8 January 2022.

21 Paolo da Col, "History of the Tartini Violin Relics," in Da Col, Airenti, Lowenberger, *The Tartini Violin Relics*, 248 ff. Perhaps this is the violin made by Bagatella himself, which Tartini's pupil Giulio Meneghini had submitted for examination to the "Accademia di Scienze, Lettere ed Arti di Padova". See Bagatella, *Regole*, 7.

22 "Li sei violini sono proveduti, e incassati a uso di lungo viaggio. Tra questi sei (tutti buoni) uno è certamente di Stainer, un altro parimenti più di Stainer, che di altro autore. La spesa (inclusa la cassetta da viaggio, e riparo della cassetta) è in tutto di zechini quaranta uno: mancano soldi pochi. In tali negozj è impossibile la precisione, quale si può dare per un violino, o per due al più: non si può dare per sei. In oltre è stato un punto di fortuna (com'è occorso nel caso presente) incontrarsi in una partita di dodeci violini tutti buoni, e questa in mano di un mio padrone, che mi ha accordato la scielta e il prezzo a mio modo. Cosiché francamente asserisco il valor intrinseco de' sei violini ascendere a molto più del prezzo assegnato. Insomma ho la consolazione di esser sicuro di aver ben servito vostra signoria illustrissima." Malagò,

Here Tartini appeared as an expert who was commissioned to make a selection of particularly good and high-quality violins from a musical and, presumably also, violin-making perspective. Since he tried to justify the price asked, it can at least be assumed that he also earned something from such a commission, as was already evident from Bagatella's information about the many instruments prepared for Tartini. If this were the case, it would be quite understandable that Tartini owned some violins only temporarily. It is not atypical for a musician who experiments with sound to become extremely attached to an instrument spontaneously and then, after a certain period of time spent in its possession, for interest to wane, leading it to being ultimately sold and perhaps replaced by another. This kind of quest is also expressed in the experiments that the violinist undertook using different thicknesses of gut strings, as documented by Fétis: "Tartini found, through experiments conducted in 1734, that the load of the four strings on the instrument was equal to 63 pounds."[23]

Tartini can certainly be considered an experienced connoisseur, probably also a lover of both old and new violins, and a man who had a great many contacts. A number of violin-making innovations took place in his sphere of influence, and in many cases, he played a decisive role in them. This was also observed by his contemporaries, as can be seen in a passage from a letter to Tartini by Gian Rinaldo Carli dated 21 August 1743: "You realised that the strings of the violin had to be thickened and the bow lengthened, as you did, in order for the vibrations to be better regulated and the sound to come out sweeter and more receptive to variations."[24]

It is clear from all the information gathered here that Giuseppe Tartini was a major contributor to bringing the technical refurbishing and sound of string instruments into line with his and the prevailing contemporary musical taste.

Bibliography

Ahrens, Christian, and Bernhard Hentrich. " 'Von einer steiner Violino daß grifbreth erhöhet...'. Tiefgreifende Reparaturen an Cremoneser und Stainer'schen Violinen in den 1730er-und 1740er-Jahren." In *Unisonus. Musikinstrumente erforschen, bewahren, sammeln*, edited by Beatrix Darmstädter and Ina Hoheisel. Vienna: Praesens, 2014.

Tartini. *Lettere e documenti*, I, 170. Translation in Malagò, *Tartini. Lettere e documenti*, II, 309.

23 "Tartini a trouvé, par des expériences faites en 1734, que la charge des quatre cordes sur l'instrument égalait 63 livres." Fétis, *Antoine Stradivari*, 92.

24 "[...] avete conosciuto doversi ingrossare le corde del violino, ed allungare l'arco, come avete fatto, perché le vibrazioni fossero più regolate, e il suono riuscisse più dolce e più suscettibile di variazioni." Malagò, *Tartini. Lettere e documenti*, I, 155. Translation in Malagò, *Tartini. Lettere e documenti*, II, 295.

Bagatella, Antonio. *Regole per la Costruzione de' Violini Viole Violoncelli e Violoni, memoria presentata all'Accademia di Scienze lettere ed arti di Padova al concorso del premio delle arti dell'anno 1782*. Padova: Zanibon, 1916.

Cacciatori, Fausto. *Antonio Stradivari. Disegni, modelli, forme*. Cremona: Fondazione del Museo del Violino Antonio Stradivari Cremona, 2016.

Curtin, Joseph. "Views on the Bridge". *The Strad* 130, no. 1555 (November 2019): 60–67.

Da Col, Paolo, Antonino Airenti and Federico Lowenberger. "The Tartini Violin Relics." *The Galpin Society Journal* 64 (2011): 248–61.

Fétis, François-Joseph. *Antoine Stradivari, Luthier Célèbre sous le Nom de Stradivarius*. Paris: Vuillaume, 1856.

Lütgendorff, Willibald Leo Freiherr von. *Die Geigen-und Lautenmacher vom Mittelalter bis zur Gegenwart*. Tutzing: Schneider, 1975.

Malagò, Laura. *Tartini. Lettere e documenti*, vol. 1. Trieste: EUT, 2020. *Discover Tartini*. Accessed 8 January 2022, https://www.discovertartini.eu/epistolario/I/.

Melkus, Eduard. *Die Violine*. Bern: Hallwag, 1975.

Montanari, Giuliana. "Conservazione e restauro degli strumenti ad arco alla corte di Firenze in epoca lorenese (1737–1770)". *Liuteria, Musica e Cultura*, edited by Renato Meucci (1997).

Antonino Airenti

The Tartini "Sound" through the Relics: Reflections and Questions Arising from the Technical and Functional Observation of Tartini Relics

Abstract: The report focuses on the author's observations and listening experiences of the bows that belonged to Tartini and of the accessories of his violin set-up, in order to reflect on the sound they could produce together and to formulate hypotheses on the timbral aesthetics of the composer. The aim is to compare the point of view of the instrumental craftsman with those of other professionals working in the musical field and to evaluate areas of possible agreement.

Keywords: Historical Informed Performance, HIP, baroque bows, snakewood, Brazil-wood, clip in frog, pike head

Introduction

Different study methods can be applied to the same subject depending on the specialization and sensitivity of each scholar. This chapter examines the possible sound desired by Tartini using the full resources of the present author's "practical" experience, his listening experiences (subjective experiences, though also shared with the musicians who frequented his workshop) and the confirmation of these experiences from the objective data of scientific studies still in progress.

The Bows

If we consider the two bows belonging to Tartini (Airenti et al. 2011), it is clear that they refer to two different periods of his life. This would also seem to be confirmed by the iconographic sources, however reliable they may be.

Fig. 1: Two bows that probably belonged to Tartini, as exhibited in the Conservatory of Music in Trieste.

The bow dating from the period of his youth is a beautiful artefact made from snakewood, elegantly faceted, with a beautiful pike-shaped head. It represents the natural evolution of the seventeenth-century models, of which it maintains certain main characteristics, including the clip-in frog and the angle created by the horse-hair and the bottom of the head. In this particular case, the wooden plug holding the horsehair inside the cavity (mortise) is also the only point of contact between the horsehair and the stick itself, a detail that makes certain playing techniques particularly easy, including the *messa di voce* and the *tremolo d'arco* that Tartini particularly loved.

Compared to its earlier models, it is considerably longer, thereby satisfying the requests of many musicians, including Tartini himself, in the first half of the eighteenth century.

In short, it is the result of a safe and consolidated project.

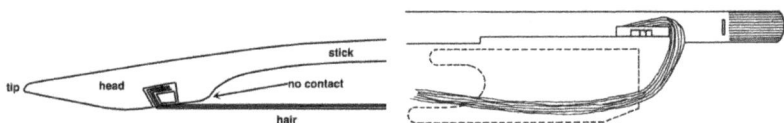

Fig.2: Section of typical seventeenth-century bow head and frog end with a clip-in tension system

On the other hand, the bow representing the "mature" Tartini features a surprising set of characteristics that make it almost unique in its kind. The swan-neck head is quite high, typical of many other bows made in the north Italian (or south German) area in the second half of the eighteenth century, and probably for this reason, the stick is made of pernambuco (or one of its congenerics). The height of the tip was almost certainly the response of the makers to the needs of musicians: specifically to perform certain bow strokes required by the contemporary repertoire more easily, including the *balzato*, and above all to play both down- and up-strokes in the same way.

The workmanship is not flawless, or perhaps it has undergone subsequent processing. The curvature is such that the bow will necessarily remain concave even under the tension of the hair.

The horsehair is secured to both ends of the stick, and there is a clip-in frog. In fact, this is the bow's most significant feature, for in a period (the second half of the eighteenth century) when all newly built bows had a screw adjustment system, this is probably the only one (or one of the very few) to feature a clip-in frog.

The difference in timbre between bows with these two different tension systems is clearly perceptible and has indeed become consolidated knowledge among musicians, as is confirmed by objective data from spectrum analyses reported in certain scientific studies (Ravina 2012; Ravina et al. 2007).

The Tailpiece and (above All) the Bridge

We do not know for sure what type of violin set-up was used by Tartini, because the instrument attributed to him has undergone many changes both internally (the bass-bar) and externally (neck replacement). But the accessories that have come down to us (especially the height of the bridge) authorize us to think that the instrument had a so-called "Classical" set-up, with the neck slightly tilted (though significantly less than in a modern set-up).

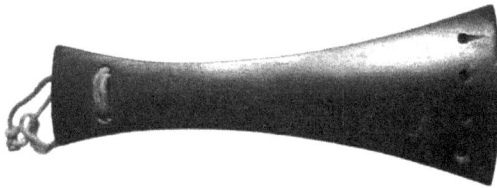

Fig.3: Tartini violin tailpiece

The tailpiece, made from maple wood with a thin ebony coating, is very elegant and has typical characteristics of the Classical period: in particular, it is considerable thinner than those of the Baroque period, and it features a much more pronounced transverse curvature. Moreover, it is much lighter than the tailpieces that came into common use in the following century.

Fig.4: Different models of historical bridges

Like the bow of the "mature" Tartini, even his bridge (presumably the last of his career) presents a surprising set of characteristics that make it almost unique. It features a substantially triangular structure like many Baroque bridges, though it is much less rigid in the upper part. The front and back surfaces are practically parallel, as in almost all the bridges of the second half of the eighteenth century. The carving design, however, is completely out of the ordinary, not to say unique.

Fig.5: Tartini violin bridge

It was from an extraordinary intuition that my colleague Federico Lowenberger made a copy of this bridge and mounted it on a violin with a Classical set-up. The subsequent listening tests carried out with many musicians showed that the sound produced by the instruments that fitted that type of bridge was decidedly different when compared to other contemporary models. In workshop practice, this bridge model has proved very useful for producing a "Baroque sound" even for musicians who have an instrument with a Classical or hybrid set-up. To date, however, no scientific data can sufficiently confirm (or refute) this observation.

The Questions

From my point of view as a craftsman who builds musical instruments, the above observations posed certain questions that in my opinion are worth reflecting on (and for which I lack the answers):

- What reason or reasons could have prompted Tartini to use a bow (and bridge) that produce a sound so sophisticatedly different from that of his contemporaries?
- Was it simply the choice of a broadminded artist open to the new playing techniques while remaining deeply attached to an earlier sound aesthetic? Or is it reasonable to think that the unusual choice of sound quality is inextricably linked to his musical style?

Acknowledgements

First of all, a special remembrance to Federico Lowenberger (1948–2013) with whom I shared 30 years of working life, friendship and study. Together we made a preliminary inspection of the Tartini relics in 2005. My thanks also go to Enrico Ravina for his readiness to help and his timely collaboration, to Paolo Da Col for granting me the honour of participating in this conference, to Rudolf Hopfner for being the first to show me the guidelines on the study of historical bows, to Renato Meucci and Gabriele Rossi Rognoni for opening the doors to so many wonderful treasures, and to Paola Parodi for the post-production of the images and her irreplaceable support on many museum visits. Finally, my thanks to all those (musicians or otherwise) who in various ways have taught me something and given me the opportunity to share it with others.

A young Tartini. Unknown 18th century Roman artist (Milano, Pinacoteca del Museo d'arte antica del Castello Sforzesco).

A mature *Tartini. Unknown 18th century artist. (Courtesy of Conservatorio di musica 'G. Tartini', Trieste)*

Bibliography

Airenti, Antonino, Paolo Da Col, and Federico Lowenberger. "The Tartini Violin Relics." *The Galpin Society Journal* LXIV (2011): 248–61.

Ravina, Enrico. "Violins Characterization through Vibro-Acoustic Experiments." *Proceedings of the Acoustics 2012 Nantes Conference*, Nantes, France. hal-00810566.

Ravina, Enrico, Federico Lowenberger, Antonino Airenti, Guido De Vecchi, and Pio Silvestri. "Violins from Baroque to Modern Mounting: An Approach to Scientific Design." *International Symposium on Musical Acoustics, ISMA2007*, Sept 2007, Barcelona.

The Sound Environment at the Basilica del Santo di Padova: Colleagues and Orchestra

Marc Vanscheeuwijck

Antonio Vandini: Tartini's Cellist, Colleague and Friend

Abstract: Invited by Giuseppe Tartini to join him in Padua, the Bolognese cellist Antonio Vandini (1690–1778) was employed at the *Cappella Musicale* of the Basilica del Santo as of 9 June 1721, and remained in his position for almost half a century, except for the four years he spent in Prague (with Tartini) from 1722 to 1726. The English music historian Charles Burney heard him play in Padua on 2 August 1770 and noticed that Vandini played "holding the bow the old-fashioned way, with the hand under it", which produces a sound that is very different from the cello as we know it.

In this chapter, I connect some of the main elements of Vandini's biography with his output as a composer for the cello, giving particular attention to the organological and technical aspects of the instrument. Vandini was a famous cellist in his day, yet today he is almost unknown and his music has been greatly neglected by cellists. He remains, however, a key figure in Italy in the transition from the Baroque to the modern cello.

Keywords: Vandini, violoncello, violotto, performance practice, cello technique, Tartini

* * *

La Sig[nor]a Chiara hà fatta la prima breccia, ed io darò l'assalto. Per la prossima festa di S. Venanzo avremo qui Tartini (ecco una Cannonata), avremo D. Antonio Vandini (ecco una Bomba) e questi sono sicuri; si spera anche di avere un bravo musico mà non è ancora sicuro, e perciò non essendo botta franca lasciamola.[1]

With this warlike metaphor, a certain Signor Trasucci from Camerino enthusiastically confirms – to Isidoro Roberti in Recanati, in a letter dated 25 April 1735, and preserved in the Conservatorio G. Tartini in Trieste – that both Giuseppe Tartini and Antonio Vandini are to perform in the service for the upcoming annual celebrations (on 18 May) of the local patron saint in the church of San Venanzio in Camerino, an important university centre and hill town in the central Marche. Don

---

1 Trasucci, Letter to Marchese Isidoro Roberti of Recanati, Camerino, 25 April 1735 (Trieste, Biblioteca del Conservatorio di Musica G. Tartini): "Signora Chiara made the first breach, and I will lead the attack. For the next feast-day of Saint Venantius we will have Tartini here (a cannon shot!), we will have D. Antonio Vandini (a bomb!) and these are guaranteed; we also hope to have a good singer, but that is not certain yet, and thus since that is not a sure bet, let us leave it at this."

Antonio Vandini's fame as a cellist thus went far beyond the Veneto and Padua, where he had been hired almost 13 years earlier. Indeed, if Vandini was considered a "weapon" even more powerful than the *Maestro delle Nazioni*, he must have been a performer of at least the level of Tartini himself, one of the most important violinists of the eighteenth century.

In recent years, Vandini has received renewed attention from both cellists and musicologists, after having been only occasionally mentioned by scholars as a musician operating in the periphery of Tartini. In his 1968 monograph on Tartini, Pierluigi Petrobelli already discussed the importance of Vandini as a colleague and close friend of Tartini's, particularly when trying to figure out the instrument for which Tartini wrote his two concertos for *viola*, an instrument now well accepted to be the cello.[2] Then, in the 1980s and around Tartini's 300th birthday in October 1992, the harpsichordist Pietro Revoltella transcribed a few compositions by Vandini and took part in performances of them in Padua. My own interest in Vandini began in 2007 with some research for a conference in Rovereto,[3] followed by an article in *Performance Practice Review* in 2008 (see Footnote 2) and another conference in Padua in 2013,[4] which convinced me that it was time to publish and perform Vandini's compositions. This eventually culminated in the realization of these two projects with cellist Elinor Frey after the 2019 conference in Trieste. In the meantime, however, several other cellists and musicologists also decided to resurrect Vandini's music, and we now have a variety of editions and recordings available.[5] This belated revival of Vandini's sonatas and concerto is probably also due to the fact that until recently the only edition of two so-called Vandini

2   Pierluigi Petrobelli, *Giuseppe Tartini. Le fonti biografiche* (Venice: Universal Edition, 1968), 26, 60, 67–9, and 72–9. Petrobelli's hypothesis that the concertos were written to the viola da gamba has now been disproved; see Marc Vanscheeuwijck, "In Search of the Eighteenth-Century 'Violoncello': Antonio Vandini and the Concertos for Viola by Tartini," *Performance Practice Review* 13 (2008): 1–20, https://doi.org/10.5642/perfpr.200813.01.07. Available at: https://scholarship.claremont.edu/ppr/vol13/iss1/7; and Bettina Hoffmann, *I bassi d'arco di Antonio Vivaldi. Violoncello, contrabbasso e viola da gamba al suo tempo e nelle sue opere* (Florence: Olschki, 2020), 120.

3   "I concerti 'per violoncello' di Giuseppe Tartini," paper delivered at the symposium *Il violino "barocco" oggi. Aspetti e problemi della prassi moderna di uno strumento antico*, Rovereto, 3 November 2007.

4   "Un virtuoso al servizio della cappella di Sant'Antonio in Padova: Antonio Vandini suonatore di violoncello," paper delivered at the *XVI Convegno internazionale sul barocco Padano (secoli XVII–XVIII)*, "Barocco Padano e musici francescani. L'apporto dei maestri Conventuali," Padua, 1–3 July 2013.

5   Recent editions: Antonio Vandini, *Six Sonatas for Violoncello and Continuo*, ed. Antonio Mostacci and Paolo Potì (Bologna: Ut Orpheus, 2018), with a preface by Antonello Manzo and Antonio Vandini, *Konzert D-Dur*, ed. Markus Möllenbeck (Magdeburg: Edition Walhall – Verlag Franz Biersack, 2015); Antonio Vandini, *Concerto in re maggiore*, ed. Gulrim Choï (Albese con Cassano: Musedita, 2015); Antonio Vandini, *6 Sonate manoscritte*, ed. Elinor Frey and Marc Vanscheeuwijck (Albese con Cassano: Musedita, 2020). There are recent recordings by Antonio

one-movement (!) sonatas for cello and piano contain not a single note by Vandini, and are indeed quite mediocre; perhaps no cellist felt inclined to dig any further into his music.[6] Availability on the internet (IMSLP) of his genuine compositions in the manuscripts located in Venice, Paris and Berlin has definitely also sparked a renewed interest.

In this chapter, I will reiterate some of the main biographical information we have on Vandini and connect it with a discussion of his output as a composer for the cello, with particular attention to the organological and technical performing aspects of the instrument.[7]

Born in Bologna on 2 November 1691, the son of Francesco Vandini, Antonio became a Franciscan friar most probably in his hometown.[8] Unfortunately, we know nothing about his upbringing or musical training. The first document that mentions him as a cellist is dated 3 April 1720: it tells us that he came from Venice and that he had been hired at the musical chapel of Santa Maria Maggiore in Bergamo.[9] Scholars have claimed that Vandini may have been a student of the famous Giuseppe Maria Jacchini, one of the cellists at San Petronio in Bologna, but that claim is unfounded. In fact, several cellists were active in Bologna around 1700, including Carlo Buffagnotti, Angelo Fiorè, Pietro Paolo and Lodovico Filippo Laurenti, Giovanni Andrea Mazza, Giovanni Broccardi, Gaetano Boni and others, all of whom could have instructed Vandini. But sometimes in our too romantic fashion, we tend to think that famous musicians must necessarily have been trained by other famous musicians.

In any case, Vandini's employment in Bergamo did not last long. On 23 August 1720, he was appointed *Maestro di Violoncello* at the Ospedale della Pietà in Venice *per qualche tempo* (for some time, beginning on 27 September), where he may have collaborated with Antonio Vivaldi.[10] He eventually resigned his post in Bergamo at the end of 1721. Vivaldi probably wrote a number of his cello concertos with Vandini's technical prowess in mind; in any case, it is from the 1720s onwards

---

Mostacci (Tactus TC692202), Elinor Frey (Passacaille PAS 1079), Francesco Galligioni (Dynamic CDS 7890), and Gaetano Nasillo (Arcana A465).

6   One sonata is in F Major and the other in G Major. They were published by Schott in Mainz (CB 48), first in an "arrangement" by Carl Schroeder in 1911 and again by Joachim Stutschewsky in 1930 (and *renewed* in 1958).

7   For further reflections on Vandini's instrument(s), see Vanscheeuwijck, *Tartini*, footnote 2, and Hoffmann, *Bassi d'arco*, 141.

8   Until recently, Vandini's birthdate was unknown, but research conducted by Antonello Manzo in the Archivio Generale Arcivescovile and in the Archivio di Stato in Bologna has revealed the exact date. See Antonello Manzo, "Antonio Vandini. Il violoncellista ai tempi di Padre Martini" (Master's thesis, Bologna, Conservatorio Statale di Musica "G .B. Martini", 2017); and Antonello Manzo, *Prefazione* to Antonio Vandini, *Six Sonatas for Violoncello and Continuo*, ed. Antonio Mostacci and Paolo Potì (Bologna: Ut Orpheus, 2018), iv.

9   Manzo, *Prefazione*, iv.

10   Manzo, *Prefazione*, v. However, there is no certainty that the two composers ever met in person.

that we find Vivaldi making greater technical demands on the cello soloist, as well as using higher registers in thumb position.[11] Given the many extant documents that grant Vandini permission to perform in churches and theatres outside Bergamo, we can surmise that he had a very active performing career throughout the Repubblica Serenissima in those years. In the meantime, having also stepped down on 4 April from his job at the Pietà in Venice, he had been unanimously appointed (by decree of 9 June 1721) as *1° violoncello* at the Veneranda Arca of the Basilica del Santo (Sant'Antonio) in Padua, where he began his duties on 1 November, on the eve of his thirtieth birthday.[12]

Vandini remained in this position – with the exception of several short-term absences – for almost half a century. On 18 June 1722, he temporarily resigned from the Veneranda Arca to move to Prague where he summoned his friend Giuseppe Tartini to join him, and where both musicians ended up being deeply involved in the colossal musical celebrations for the coronation of the Habsburg Emperor Charles VI as King of Bohemia in June 1723. Along with Tartini, Vandini was subsequently hired in the service of Count Ferdinand Franz Kinsky in Prague, but both musicians decided to return to Padua in the spring of 1726, where they were restored to their former positions by 1 June.[13] Apart from the invitation to Camerino in 1735 mentioned in the letter opening this essay, Vandini seems to have performed at the papal court on 22 May 1736.[14] We know of one other documented absence, for the celebration of the feast-day of Saint Francis (4 October) in the Basilica di San Francesco in Assisi in 1750 (where he performed with violinist Carlo Tessarini),[15] after which he continued his journey to Rome. That is where Pier Leone Ghezzi drew a couple of caricatures of him and of his nephew Don Ludovico Vandini between 21 and 23 October 1750, portraying Antonio holding the bow with underhand grip (see Fig. 1).[16] Otherwise, it is a fact that until the middle of the century, Vandini also often travelled – always with Tartini, but also with oboe virtuoso Matteo Bissoli and maestro di cappella Antonio Vallotti – to perform in various churches and theatres throughout Italy.[17]

---

11 For example, the concertos RV 400, 401, 411, 413, 418 and 424 are particularly demanding technically and could be situated chronologically in the 1720s and 1730s. See Hoffmann, *Bassi d'arco*, 314–83.

12 See Petrobelli, *Tartini*, 67, footnote 3.

13 Petrobelli, *Tartini*, 26, and footnote 5; information from Francesco Fanzago, *Orazione del Signor Abate Francesco Fanzago Padovano delle lodi di Giuseppe Tartini recitata nella Chiesa dei RR. PP. Serviti in Padova Li 31. Di Marzo 1770* (Padua: Conzatti, 1770), 33, footnote 21.

14 See Giancarlo Rostirolla, *Il "Mondo novo" musicale di Pier Leone Ghezzi* (Milano: Skira, 2001), 414.

15 See Manzo, *Prefazione*, vi.

16 Rostirolla, *Mondo novo*, 228–29, and 414–15; and Fig. 1: Drawing by Pier Leone Ghezzi, Fossombrone, Biblioteca Comunale Passionei, Album di caricature del Ghezzi, n. 53. The text reads: *D. Antonio Vandini Famoso sonatore di Violoncello al servizio della Capella di S. Antonio in Padova fatto da me Cavalier Ghezzi.*

17 See Manzo, *Prefazione*, vi.

Fig. 1: *Drawing by Pier Leone Ghezzi, Antonio Vandini* (Fossombrone, Biblioteca Comunale Passionei, Album di caricature del Ghezzi, n. 53)

Following the death of his life-long colleague and friend Tartini in February 1770, at almost 79 Vandini resigned his position in June of the same year, ensuring that he was replaced by his former student, cellist Giuseppe Callegari. Although Vandini's petition, preserved in the archives of the Basilica del Santo in Padua, is not dated, Petrobelli supposes that it was presented on 10 May 1770:

Io d[on] Antonio Vandini [...] riverentemente suplico per ottenere grazia à benefizio di d[omin]o Giuseppe Callegari Suonatore di Violoncello e mio Scolaro il quale da molti anni serve quest'insigne Capella per Sopranumerario senza alcun stipendio, e spero che sarà dalla loro carità, e giustizia beneficato di qualche stabile stipendio per animarlo à continuare con feruore, ed assiduità nel Servitio del glorioso Santo senza procurarsi impiego in altro luogo. Potevo godere delle beneficenze accordatemi da questa Religiosa, e Nobile Presidenza con la giubilazione segnatami riguardo alla avanzata mia età, ed al lungo servizio, che comincia dall'anno 1721, e pure mi sforzo à continuare quanto mi posso in Orchestra p[er] non abusarmi della grazia ricevuta, e contribuisco al sud[dett]o Giuseppe Callegari ducati 50 del mio Onorario, acciò si

facia corraggio di continuare nell'esercizio di questa insigne Capella, e nutrisca una
vera speranza d'essere ammesso con stabilità, ed onorario.[18]

Six years later, Vandini moved back to Bologna, where he lived in the parish of
Santa Maria della Mascarella, and died on 18 May 1778.[19]

In addition to his frequent concert tours with his colleagues, Vandini was first
cellist in the Basilica del Santo in Padua, where his duties included playing during
regular Mass and Compline services on Sundays and Mass on Tuesdays, to which
obviously all the important moveable feasts throughout the liturgical year need to
be added. It is also during such liturgical services (sometimes extensive) that concertos were performed, along with liturgical vocal-and-instrumental compositions
in *concertato* style. The English music historian Charles Burney visited Padua in
summer 1770 and for Thursday, 2 August he reports the following:

> [...] I went to St. Anthony's church, where, it being *the Day of Pardon*, there was
> a mass, with solo verses of *Padre Valloti*'s composition who was there to beat the
> time; [...] I wanted much to hear the celebrated hautbois Matteo Bissioli [*sic*], and
> the famous old Antonio Vandini, on the violoncello, who, the Italians say, plays and
> expresses *a parlare*, that is, in such a manner as to make his instrument speak; but nei-
> ther of these performers had solo parts. However, I give them credit for great abilities,
> as they are highly extolled by their countrymen, who must, by the frequent hearing
> of excellent performers of all kinds, insensibly become good judges of musical merit.
> People accustomed to bad music, may be pleased by it; but those, on the contrary,
> who have been long used to good music, and performers, *cannot*. It was remarkable

---

18 Padua, Archivio Antico della Veneranda Arca del Santo, Busta 128, cited by Petrobelli,
    Tartini, 73, footnote 1: "I, Don Antonio Vandini [...] reverently plead to obtain favour
    for Don Giuseppe Callegari, cello player and my student, who has for many years
    served in this illustrious Chapel as a supernumerary without any payment, and
    I hope that he will through your charity and justice be the beneficiary of some stable
    stipend to motivate him to continue, with fervour and assiduity, in the service of
    the glorious Santo without taking a position in another place. I was able to reap the
    benefit of the generosity shown me by this religious and noble *presidenza* with the
    pension accorded me for my advanced age and long service which began in the year
    1721, and yet I drive myself to continue in the Orchestra for as long as I can so as not
    to abuse the favour I have received, and I contribute to the abovementioned Giuseppe
    Callegari fifty ducats of my honorarium, so that he may be inspired to continue in
    the service of this illustrious Chapel, and may nourish a legitimate hope of being
    admitted here with both security and honorarium."
19 The announcement of Vandini's death was read at the meeting of the Presidenti
    dell'Arca in Padua on 23 May 1778: "Letta la notizia della morte, avvenuta a Bologna,
    di Don Antonio Vandini violoncello, e volendo la Presidenza dare dimostrazione
    della memoria che conserva di lui, fu stabilito all'unanimità di rilasciare ai suoi eredi
    l'intero trimestre che scadrà il 30 giugno prossimo." See Manzo, *Prefazione*, vii.

that Antonio [Vandini], and all the other violoncello players here, hold the bow in the old-fashioned way, with the hand under it.[20]

On the subject of holding the bow in underhand position, Burney is not the only person to remark on this. In his article *Entwurf eines Verzeichnisses der besten jetztlebenden Tonkünstler in Europa* Christoph Gottlieb von Murr confirms it as well:

> Der berühmte Antonio Vandini. Er halt den Bogen nach der alten Art, mit der Hand am Haare und dem Daumen am Holze, wie bey dem Gambenspiele.[21]

Indeed, Vandini and his colleagues in Padua may well have been some of the last players to use the bow in the typically Baroque Italian underhand grip, which profoundly alters articulation and phrasing compared to the overhand bow grip most "Baroque" cellists use today.[22]

All we have left of Vandini's compositional output are six sonatas for cello and basso continuo from different periods in his career. The earliest piece is also the only one precisely dated: the Sonata in C Major, preserved in Venice and dated May 1717.[23] Two more sonatas, one in B-flat Major and one in A Minor, are preserved in Paris;[24] they are part of a manuscript of sonatas compiled in 1730, though the compositions probably also belong to Vandini's early creative period in Venice, Bergamo and Prague (i.e., between c.1715 and c.1726), along with one of the Berlin sonatas, the Sonata in C Major.[25] The last two sonatas, one in B-flat Major and one in E Major, both extant in Berlin, seem on purely stylistic and cello-technical grounds to belong to a much later creative period, sometime between 1750 and 1770.[26]

Finally, Vandini also left us a Concerto in D Major for violoncello solo, two violins, viola and basso continuo, which survives in a manuscript in the Landesbibliothek Mecklenburg-Vorpommern in Schwerin, and is probably datable between the Paris sonatas and the later Berlin sonatas, also in comparison with the style of the two

---

20 Charles Burney, *The Present State of Music in France and Italy* (London: T. Becket and Co, 1773), 140–42.

21 Christoph Gottlieb von Murr, "Entwurf eines Verzeichnisses der besten jetztlebenden Tonkünstler in Europa," *Journal zur Kunstgeschichte und zur allgemeinen Literatur*, II (1776): 1–30, 23: "The famous Antonio Vandini. He holds the bow in the old fashion, with the hand on the hair and the thumb on the stick, as in gamba playing."

22 In their recent aforementioned CD recordings, Elinor Frey and also Francesco Galligioni use underhand bowing, see Footnote 5. See also Marc Vanscheeuwijck, "Violoncello and other Bass Violins in Baroque Italy," in *Gli esordi del violoncello a Napoli e in Europa*, ed. Dinko Fabris (Barletta: Cafagna, 2020), 25–100, especially 39.

23 I-Vnm, Mss. It.IV.1095, catalogued Van.1 in Elinor Frey's and my proposal of a chronology of Vandini's seven compositions based on stylistic and cello technical features.

24 F-Pn, Vm⁷-6285 (resp. Van. 3 & 4).

25 D-B, KHM 5528 (Van. 2).

26 D-B, KHM 5527 & KHM 5529 (resp. Van. 6 & 7).

concertos which Giuseppe Tartini wrote for Vandini.[27] Intriguing are also the fingerings that appear in the solo part in a few movements of the two later Berlin sonatas. At first they seem awkward, but upon closer examination, they make good sense, and adopting them strictly forces the cellist to alter certain fingering techniques that are now considered modern. On the other hand, we have no proof that these fingerings were actually Vandini's; they may have been added later in the manuscript by a cellist who performed them in Berlin, in the late eighteenth or early nineteenth century. In any case, they offer an approach to fingering that is much more *stable*, in which the cellist avoids unnecessary position changes: once the left hand is placed on the fingerboard with the thumb as a *capotasto*, it stays put as long as possible, making much more use of string crossings than we do in modern cello technique.[28]

Another significant issue is the question of the instrument. What type of cello did Vandini play? And did he use the same sort of instrument throughout his long career? As is now well known, the cello, even what today we call the Baroque cello, was not standardized in its current form, size and playing technique until the 1740s, likely under the influence of Neapolitan cellists active in Paris. Considering that Vandini held on to older-style bowing techniques, he might also have kept the habit of using smaller-than-modern violoncellos for his solo work (and larger ones for *ripieno* or accompaniment, i.e., orchestral playing), though certainly strung with four strings, not five as has occasionally been claimed.[29] We have no way of knowing this, except that the fingerings and the passagework in the Venice and Berlin sonatas demonstrate a well-developed use of the so-called thumb position, necessary for playing the many pitches and passages around or above the middle of the string, thus indicating a four-string instrument tuned C-g-d-a. A five-string cello is unlikely, though not entirely to be excluded for the earliest sonatas (Van. 1–3) – especially if played by less virtuoso amateurs – but on a four-string cello, the use of the thumb as a *capotasto* is necessary in several sonatas, particularly the last three and the concerto (Van. 4–7). Since the Venice sonata (Van. 1) is dated

---

27 D-SWI, Mus. 4736/4 (Van. 5); see Vanscheeuwijck, *Tartini.*

28 See also Bettina Hoffmann's considerations on Vandini's fingerings in Hoffmann, *Bassi d'arco*, 174–77.

29 We know that in the Venetian Republic, cellists had instruments made not only by local luthiers (e.g. Matteo Goffriller, Domenico Montagnana, Santo Serafin, Pietro Guarneri, etc.) but also by Cremonese (Stradivari) and other Northern Italian makers. It is striking that in the 1720–30s, various builders (including Stradivari himself) also made several cellos of a rather smaller size, with sound case lengths between 69 cm and 74 cm, whereas the measurements were later stabilized around 75 cm. However, case lengths do not tell us everything about vibrating string lengths, which are the real issue here, because the position of the bridge (often still at the bottom of the F-holes at the time) and varying neck lengths were also determinative. See Stewart Pollens, *Stradivari* (Cambridge: Cambridge University Press, 2010), 84–85, and Hoffmann, *Bassi d'arco*, 151–63.

as early as 1717, and the use of the thumb though not absolutely essential is very likely, it could indeed antedate by at least a couple of decades the first attested use of the thumb position.

On the other hand, in this case as well, some reconsideration of accepted knowledge about the use of the thumb as a *capotasto* is in order here. Michel Corrette was the first to describe it in his method in 1741, causing modern Baroque cellists to be hesitant to use it in earlier repertoires.[30] One way to avoid the use of the thumb in high positions on a four-string instrument is to use a five-string violoncello (possibly tuned C/D-G-a-d'/e'), which was attested in most areas of Europe in the seventeenth century. However, when Neapolitan cellists such as Francesco Paolo Alborea (*il Francischiello*), Francesco Supriani and Salvatore Lanzetti, and Roman cellists such as Giovanni Battista Costanzi began to acquire notoriety, thanks to their virtuoso compositions for the cello; or when Vivaldi (among others)[31] produced his most virtuosic concertos a couple of decades before Corrette's method appeared in print, the use of the thumb seems to be both unavoidable and frequently used on a four-string instrument already in the 1720s. Of course, when we consider cello technique through the playing of top-quality professional virtuosi only, such advanced features seem natural, but in the growing eighteenth-century world of amateur musicians, thumb position might be (as it still is today!) too uncomfortable for the larger crowd of average-quality players. Since there is no way to ascertain the existence of five-string instruments in Naples, Rome or Venice from the 1720s on – in fact, they were probably no longer used by professional cellists at that point – it is fairly certain that cello virtuosi did indeed use thumb position already in the 1720s or slightly earlier.[32]

Yet another element is the existence of smaller-type violoncellos – not tenor violas, which were tuned like an alto viola (in c-g-d'-a'), but small bass violins with four strings tuned a fifth higher than the modern cello (G-d-a-e'); these were in use particularly in the latter part of the eighteenth century. Indeed, there are several compositions (and not only in the Italian peninsula) that would require thumb position on a four-string modern cello and that never use the bottom string: in such cases, thumb position is not necessary, since the cellist can easily play pitches up to g" in regular positions on the high-pitched instrument. This

---

30 Michel Corrette, *Methode, théorique et pratique. Pour Apprendre en peu de tems le Violoncelle dans sa Perfection* (Paris, 1741), 41: "Chapitre XIII. En quelle occasion on doit se servir du pouce, et de la maniere de jouer les dessus sur le violoncelle" ("In which occasions one needs to use the thumb, and on the manner of playing treble parts on the cello").
31 As other composers, cellists or not, we could add the Roman Nicola Francesco Haym; the Neapolitans Giuseppe De Majo, Leonardo Leo, and Nicola Fiorenza; and the Venetians Fortunato Chelleri, Andrea Zani, and Giovanni Perroni; see Hoffmann, *Bassi d'arco*, 117–19.
32 See also Hoffmann, *Bassi d'arco*, 137–44.

might be the instrument that was referred to with the term *violotto*, which often appears in the documents from Padua in connection with Vandini.[33] As is now clear too, the term *viola* in Naples and in Venice normally refer to a *basso viola* or larger cello (violone), while *violoncello* or *violoncino* – and in some of J.S. Bach's sacred compositions, *violoncello piccolo* – referred to smaller instruments. The term *violot[t]o*, however, seems to be found primarily in the Venetian Republic and in areas where Venetian influence was strong, like the Marches.[34] One such example of the use of *violotto* is in a 1797 concerto for violotto (even called *lira*), horn and orchestra by Emanuele Nappi (1767–1836), the dilettante composer from Polverigi (province of Ancona), which is clearly intended for a four-string small cello, most probably tuned G-d-a-e' with an ambitus from G to g#".[35]

Although it was still customary for late eighteenth-century professional cellists to have a smaller instrument for solo performances and a larger one for orchestral playing,[36] there is no tangible proof to ascertain that they were tuned differently from the by then standardized C-G-d-a-tuning, or that Vandini played instruments of different sizes. The fact that he was sometimes referred to as a player of the viola or violoncello, and sometimes of the violotto, could be an indication in that direction, if we accept that these different terms indeed denote different sizes of instruments and/or different tunings, which is not necessarily the case. In addition, in all Vandini's compositions, whether they dwell in the highest registers or not, the (sometimes very occasional) use of the low C string is always required. Only in the 1717 sonata from Venice (Van. 1) does Vandini almost completely avoid the C string: he prescribes a low C three times in C Major chords in which that low C also appears in the basso continuo line. In essence, the C string here is thus not absolutely necessary, meaning that it could possibly be played on a small instrument tuned in G-d-a-e', as is also the case in both concertos by Tartini, and in other concertos such as those by Nicola Antonio Porpora or Nicola Sabatino.[37] In any case, and to conclude these reflections on instruments and playing technique, it is most probable that Vandini played a smaller-than-standard cello for all his solo

---

33 See Petrobelli, *Tartini*, 72–79, and Vanscheeuwijck, *Tartini*, footnote 24.
34 There is also a *Sonata X.^{ma} p[er] il Violotto* and basso continuo in A Major by Vero-nese composer Evaristo Felice Dall'Abaco preserved in Vienna (A-Wn, E.M. 18), see Robert Haas, *Die Estensischen Musikalien. Thematisches Verzeichnis mit Einleitung* (Regensburg: Bosse Verlag, 1927), 75–6, and Hoffmann, *Bassi d'arco*, 149, foot-note 474.
35 The autograph manuscript is preserved in the Biblioteca Comunale Luciano Benincasa in Ancona, along with several Paduan manuscript copies of concertos and sonatas by Tartini. See Gabriele Moroni, ed., *La musica negli archivi e nelle biblioteche delle Marche* (Fiesole: Nardini, 1996), 37–8. I should add that even on a small instrument tuned G-d-a'-e', thumb position is occasionally necessary.
36 As we know from Quantz and Boccherini; see Vanscheeuwijck, "Violoncello and other Bass Violins", 41–2.
37 See Vanscheeuwijck, *Tartini*, 17–9.

sonatas, that he played it with underhand bow grip, and that he was quite profi-cient in his use of left-hand thumb technique during his entire career. If Pier Leone Ghezzi portrayed Vandini playing the instrument with underhand bowing, and with his left hand clearly placed high up on the fingerboard and in thumb position, it probably means that these two elements were distinctive features of his playing technique as an exceptional virtuoso.

Finally, in terms of style, all of Vandini's compositions for cello can be situated within a general galant-style idiom typical of Northern Italy between roughly 1720 and 1770. As the sonatas evolve, however, Baroque characteristics give way to more classical elements, while technical demands generally become more rigorous over time. Compared to the rather late-Baroque Venice sonata of 1717 (Van. 1), the two Paris sonatas display a stylistic language that is definitely more galant and thus probably slightly later, most likely to be situated in the 1730s. The opening *Largo* of the A Minor Sonata (Van. 4) is a *Siciliana* with elaborate ornaments through scales in 16th (semiquavers) and 32nd notes (demisemiquavers); the subsequent *Allegro* displays a long passage in arpeggios *all'8va [alta]* and chords in 16th notes, combined with triplets in a typical galant style. The concluding *Allegro assai* finale is extremely short with its 16 measures in 3/8, recalling some Neapolitan sonatas by Pergolesi and Scarlatti, and concertos by Leo. On the other hand, the Sonata in B-flat Major (Van. 3), also in three movements, has a narrower ambitus (D to e-flat"), though most of the composition stays within G and d". It opens with a *Largo* in *Siciliana*-style as well, though it is less elaborate than the A Minor sonata. Here too, Vandini wrote several passages in the bass clef *all'ottava alta*; there are large leaps in the *Allegro*; and the final *Minuet* in 3/8 is again quite elaborate in its ornaments. This sonata is definitely a later composition than the Venice sonata (Van. 1), through probably earlier than the A Minor Paris sonata (Van. 4).

Again based on stylistic elements and on its cello-technical features, we could possibly place the Concerto in D Major (Van. 5) between 1740 and 1750. Here too, the pitch extension does not exceed d", though several passages dwell around a', including the 16th-note (semiquaver) *batteries* in double stops, i.e., on the middle of the a-string of the cello, thus clearly requiring the occasional use of the thumb as a *capotasto*.

Among the three Berlin sonatas, the last set of compositions by Vandini, the C Major (Van. 2) has the most characteristics of the earlier galant style, sim-ilar to those of the Concerto (Van. 5) or to some of the sacred compositions that include *obbligato* cello parts by Francesco Vallotti, and should be dated some-time in the 1730s, like the Paris sonatas.[38] In this sonata with its three movements (*Andante – Allegro – Allegro*), the low C string is never used, and thumb posi-tion is not required anywhere, while the technical demands are quite limited: no double stops or complex arpeggios, and the large leaps and few upward reaches

---

38 For example, Vallotti's *Nisi Dominus* (1727), the various *Ecce nunc* (of 1730, 1731, 1734, and 1740), the two *Gloria* (1731 and 1732), etc.

to c" are very comfortable: it is undoubtedly the easiest piece of Vandini's output. Completely different, however, are the other two sonatas: the E Major Sonata (Van. 7), copied in the treble clef (always to be read an octave lower) and bass clef, offers the listener an almost classical-style idiom. A lyrical opening *Grave* precedes two *Allegro* movements filled with double stops, chords, fast passage work in 16th notes (semiquavers) and occasional *bariolages*. As mentioned before, this sonata has been provided with extremely illuminating fingerings (perhaps by Vandini) that often require the use of the thumb as a *capotasto* and prove that high positions were used even on the lower strings so as to maintain a stable place of the left hand, thereby minimizing large position changes on the fingerboard. Chronologically, this appears to be the latest of Vandini's sonatas.

Lastly, the Sonata in B-flat Major (Van. 6), also copied utilizing the "French tenor clef" or treble clef to be read an octave lower, and with the same movement layout as the E Major sonata, is almost comparable to Luigi Boccherini's cello sonatas of the late 1760s and early 1770s, both stylistically and in terms of cello technique. With its ambitus of three octaves and a fourth (C to f"), its numerous double stops and fast passage work, its extensive and essential use of thumb position as indicated by the fingerings, this piece is clearly also conceived for the "classical" four-string cello, though still played with underhand bow grip.

In conclusion, I should reiterate that the chronology I have proposed here is entirely based on stylistic trends in Vandini's seven compositions in combination with purely cello-technical considerations. Distributed over his long career (1717–70), these few pieces for cello unfortunately make up his entire (extant) compositional output, and there are no indications as to the contexts and venues in which they could have been performed. Possibly, his concert tours with Tartini, Bissoli and Vallotti may have included occasions to perform them, whereas the concerto was probably intended for the liturgy at the Basilica del Santo in Padova where he spent almost five decades of his career alongside his close friend and colleague, Giuseppe Tartini. However, through the sonatas and the concerto of such an eminent cello virtuoso as Antonio Vandini – comparable to someone like Salvatore Lanzetti in Naples who introduced the cello as a virtuoso solo instrument in Turin, Paris and London – we can see that the dramatic evolution and transformation of cello technique that was occurring between 1720 and 1770 happened in Padua as well, and was not the hallmark solely of the most important European capitals.

Bibliography

Burney, Charles. *The Present State of Music in France and Italy*. London: T. Becket and Co, 1773.

Corrette, Michel. *Methode, théorique et pratique. Pour Apprendre en peu de tems le Violoncelle dans sa Perfection*. Paris, 1741.

Fanzago, Francesco. *Orazione del Signor Abate Francesco Fanzago Padovano delle lodi di Giuseppe Tartini recitata nella Chiesa dei RR. PP. Serviti in Padova Li 31. Di Marzo 1770*. Padua: Conzatti, 1770.

Haas, Robert. *Die Estensischen Musikalien. Thematisches Verzeichnis mit Einleitung.* Regensburg: Bosse Verlag, 1927.

Hoffmann, Bettina. *I bassi d'arco di Antonio Vivaldi. Violoncello, contrabbasso e viola da gamba al suo tempo e nelle sue opere.* Florence: Olschki, 2020.

Manzo, Antonello. "Antonio Vandini. Il violoncellista ai tempi di Padre Martini." Master's thesis, Bologna, Conservatorio Statale di Musica G.B. Martini, 2017.

Manzo, Antonello. *Prefazione* to Antonio Vandini, *Six Sonatas for Violoncello and Continuo.* Edited by Antonio Mostacci and Paolo Potì. Bologna: Ut Orpheus, 2018.

Moroni, Gabriele, ed. *La musica negli archivi e nelle biblioteche delle Marche.* Fiesole: Nardini, 1996.

Murr, Christoph Gottlieb von. "Entwurf eines Verzeichnisses der besten jetztlebenden Tonkünstler in Europa." *Journal zur Kunstgeschichte und zur allgemeinen Literatur* II (1776): 1–30.

Petrobelli, Pierluigi. *Giuseppe Tartini. Le fonti biografiche.* Venice: Universal Edition, 1968.

Pollens, Stewart. *Stradivari.* Cambridge: Cambridge University Press, 2010.

Rostirolla, Giancarlo. *Il "Mondo novo" musicale di Pier Leone Ghezzi.* Milano: Skira, 2001.

Trasucci. Letter to Marchese Isidoro Roberti of Recanati, Camerino, 25 April 1735. Trieste, Biblioteca del Conservatorio di Musica G. Tartini.

Vandini, Antonio. *Concerto in re maggiore.* Edited by Gulrim Choï. Albese con Cassano: Musedita, 2015.

Vandini, Antonio. *Konzert D-Dur.* Edited by Markus Möllenbeck. Magdeburg: Edition Walhall – Verlag Franz Biersack, 2015.

Vandini, Antonio. *Six Sonatas for Violoncello and Continuo.* Edited by Antonio Mostacci and Paolo Potì. Bologna: Ut Orpheus, 2018, with a preface by Antonello Manzo.

Vandini, Antonio. *6 Sonate manoscritte.* Edited by Elinor Frey and Marc Vanscheeuwijck. Albese con Cassano: Musedita, 2020.

Vanscheeuwijck, Marc. "In Search of the Eighteenth-Century 'Violoncello': Antonio Vandini and the Concertos for Viola by Tartini." *Performance Practice Review* 13 (2008): 1–20. https://doi.org/10.5642/perfpr.200 813.01.07. Available at: https://scholarship.claremont.edu/ppr/vol13/iss1/7

Vanscheeuwijck, Marc. "Violoncello and other Bass Violins in Baroque Italy." In *Gli esordi del violoncello a Napoli e in Europa*, edited by Dinko Fabris, 25–100. Barletta: Cafagna, 2020.

Alfredo Bernardini

Matteo Bissoli, Tartini's Oboist Colleague

Abstract: Along with violinist Tartini, cellist Vandini and organist Vallotti, the oboist Matteo Bissoli (1712–80) from Brescia played an important role in the musical life of Padua in the mid-eighteenth century. Bissoli was appointed to the *cappella* of S. Antonio in Padua in 1736 and kept that post until his death. He gave solo concerts also in other Italian towns and enjoyed an international reputation, as proved by the chronicles of Jerome de Lalande and Charles Burney. Only very few complete compositions by Bissoli have survived. Among these is a sonata that is one of the earliest pieces to extend the range of the oboe up to f³. Bissoli's oboe, as shown in his printed portrait and in other iconography, was apparently a particular model with a straight outer profile that was common only in the region of Venice.

Keywords: Bissoli, oboe

Unquestionably, what is most often remembered about musical life in eighteenth-century Italy is the excellence of its stringed instruments: both the activities of the age's leading luthiers and the presence of charismatic violinists such as Corelli, Vivaldi, Tartini and many others.

And though it is true that eighteenth-century wind instruments are more typically considered as French (on account of their origin) or, secondly, as German (in view of the attention devoted to them by Telemann, Bach and Handel); nonetheless, as we move towards the middle of the century, we encounter certain wind instrumentalist-composers in Italy who contributed to a fresh development of their instruments and their repertoire. After the highly talented virtuoso Giuseppe Sammartini, son of the French oboist Alexis Saint Martin and brother of Giovanni Battista ("inventor of the Classical symphony"), it fell to the Besozzi family to disseminate a new oboe throughout Europe. This was an instrument that still had two keys, but with a narrower bore and a more penetrating sound than the preceding French model: an instrument today often referred to as the "Classical oboe" by modern players. The most authoritative member of the Besozzi family was Alessandro, who was born in Parma, worked in Turin alongside Pugnani and lived for a good 91 years from 1702 to 1793. Today we know of around a hundred trio sonatas, various sonatas and a few concertos by Besozzi.

The oboist closest to Tartini, however, is Matteo Bissoli. Bissoli was born in Brescia on 13 May 1712. Nothing is known of his training, but his participation in the musical life of the city, which at the time was part of the Republic of Venice, is

documented from 1729 to 1737. On 28 December 1736, he was engaged as oboist of
the *cappella* at Il Santo in Padua. On this occasion, we read the following comment
about him: "a virtuoso well-known and of great merit ... an excellent player of the
oboe who may make this illustrious *cappella* more ornate, no less for the proper
execution of *concerti* than for the singularity of his person".[1] Bissoli's starting
salary at Il Santo was 150 *ducati*, but it was soon raised to 170, thus equalling that
of the first violinist Giuseppe Tartini. His name appears in the documents alongside those of Tartini, Padre Vallotti and the cellist Antonio Vandini. In a letter of
21 August 1751, Vallotti, referring to Bissoli, Tartini and Vandini, writes: "Three
personalities of such a nature make the whole orchestra stand out."[2]

An interesting letter from Tartini to Padre Martini, dated 23 June 1752, bears
witness to the attachment and regard that the writer felt for his oboist colleague: "I
am obliged to pass on the news that in the rooms of our Padre Maestro Vallotti, the
trial of the third sound was carried out, with two oboes played, one by our famous
Signor Bissoli and the other by a student of his. The third sound is detected a lot
better than from two violins, and it is the very same as that resulting from two
violins."[3]

---

1   "virtuoso ben noto e di molto merito... eccellente suonator d'oboè che rendesse più
     ornata questa illustre cappella, non meno per il giusto compimento de' concerti, che
     per la singolarità del soggetto".
2   Leonardo Frasson, "Francescantonio Vallotti maestro di cappella nella Basilica del
     Santo," *Il Santo*, xx series ii (1980): 297.
3   "Ho debito di avanzarle la notizia, che in stanza del nostro Padre Maestro Vallotti si
     è fatta la prova del terzo suono con due oboe suonati, uno dal nostro famoso Signor
     Bissoli, e l'altro da un di lui scolare. Il terzo suono si rileva molto meglio che da due
     violini, et è lo stesso identico, che risulta da due violini." Giuseppe Tartini, *Lettere
     e documenti*, ed. Giorgia Malagò, I: 225: http://www.discovertartini.eu/epistolario/
     I/224/

Fig.1: Giuseppe Tirabosco, *Portrait of Matteo Bissoli* (1712–1780), engraving, Padua ca.1776. From the author's collection.

Bissoli is also mentioned in two letters of November and December 1741 from Padre Vallotti to Giordano Riccati (1709–90), mathematician and physicist from the Veneto region, on the acoustic experiments that also involved the oboist: Vallotti attests that Bissoli succeeds in obtaining the notes of a hexachord with a single reed (without the oboe) but would be capable of producing up to an octave with a better reed.

Bissoli was granted permission to be absent from Padua on various occasions, in 1738, 1740, 1742 and 1744, to play in concerts in the theatres of Genoa and Vicenza. From a letter he sent to Padre Martini on 17 July 1779, we learn that he also played in Bologna: on this occasion, he received a relic of St Antony as a fee and he despairs at having lost it.

Bissoli's reputation extended outside Italy and various musical travellers wished to visit him and hear him play, among whom Jerome de Lalande in 1766 and Charles Burney in 1770. The esteem in which he was held in Italy is curiously documented in a printed portrait of his pupil Domenico Scolari (fl. 1763–1802), which carries the caption "the only one who, for sensitivity and sweetness, can legitimately be called a pupil of the immortal Bissoli".[4] It is worth noting that the image includes scores by Bissoli and Tartini.

Fig.2: Ignazio Colombo, *Portrait of Domenico Scolari* (1763–1802), engraving, Trieste 1789. Milan, Civica Raccolta delle Stampe Achille Bertarelli.

---

4   "Dominicus Scolari, Immortalis Bissoli alumnus, Suavitate et dulcedine numerari licet unicus".

Bissoli died in Padua on 21 February 1780 of pulmonary emphysema, a bachelor living with his sister and father. He was soon succeeded, in May 1780, by Pietro Ferlendis (1748–1836), brother of the better-known Giuseppe.

Few of Bissoli's works have survived. Among them is a Sonata for oboe and continuo in G Minor at the library of the Conservatorio di Genova, which is perhaps the first piece to extend the range of the oboe up to f [3]. Apart from this, we know of a Sonata for strings in F Major preserved at the Fondazione Levi in Venice, a Concerto for oboe in D Major at the Conservatorio di Venezia (for which unfortunately the solo part is missing), a Trio Sonata in D Major dated 1751 (again lacking one part, that of the second oboe or violin) at the Archivio del Comune of Gorizia and a curious *Solfeggio* in C Major for unspecified upper voice (in soprano C clef, but without text) and continuo at the Library of Rostock, that looks like an instrumental sonata, but goes too low for the oboe range. But it is likely that he once had a (today lost) library that was full of his own concertos (since it is known that Bissoli often performed his own concertos for oboe) and that perhaps also included oboe concertos by his colleagues Tartini, Vandini and Vallotti. In the Library of Il Santo are preserved various arias on sacred texts by Padre Vallotti with interesting obligato parts for the oboe, very likely written to be performed by Bissoli. Other composers writing for the same chapel, among whom Francesco Maria Zuccari, devoted virtuosic parts to the oboe, probably with Bissoli in mind.

Lastly, in the following lines a brief comment on the particular type of oboe used by Bissoli is analyzed. It was a model from the Veneto area of which very few examples have survived. In appearance, it is distinguished by the simplicity of its completely straight outer profile with brass ferrules. While this oboe is barely sketched in the portraits of Bissoli and Scolari, of much greater detail is the painting by Sebastiano Lazzari of 1752, which shows an oboe of this type and even includes its reed: information that is always extremely valuable for those in the trade.

Fig.3: Sebastiano Lazzari, *Trompe-l'oeil with musical instruments, score for harpsichord, painting with rhinoceros and lottery receipt*, Verona 1752. Finarte Auction Sale in Rome 30 May 2023.

Fig.4: Matteo Bissoli, Sonata for Oboe in g minor, Manuscript, Conservatory of Music "N. Paganini", Genoa, SS.B1.1.10c

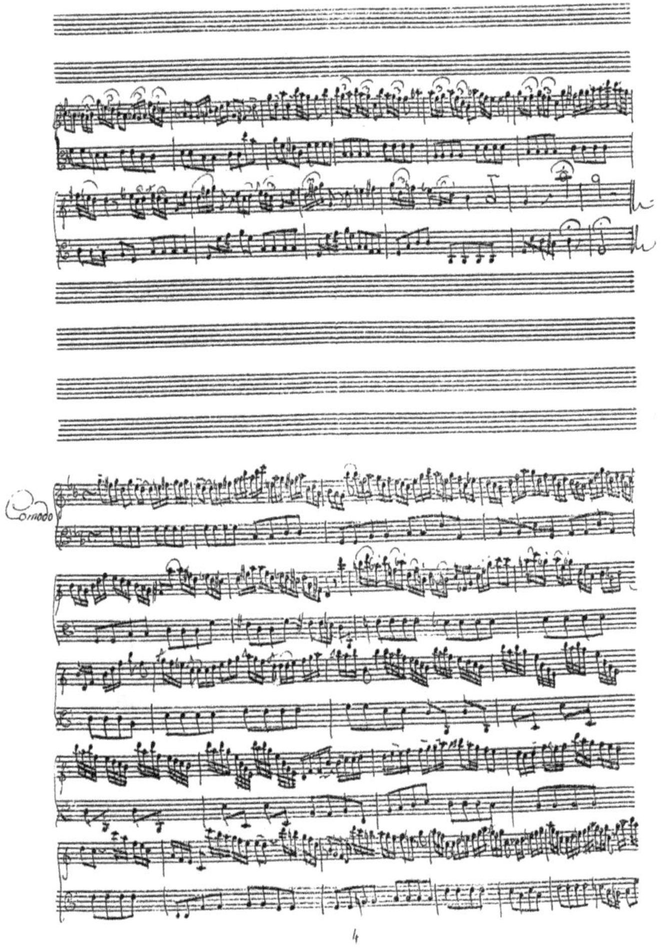

Fig.4: Continued

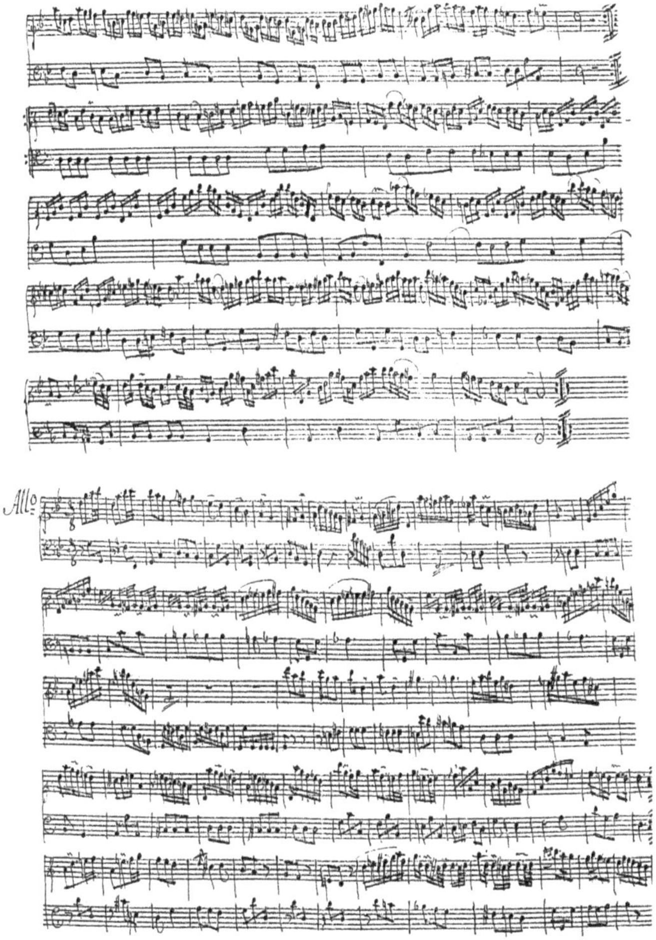

Fig.4: Continued

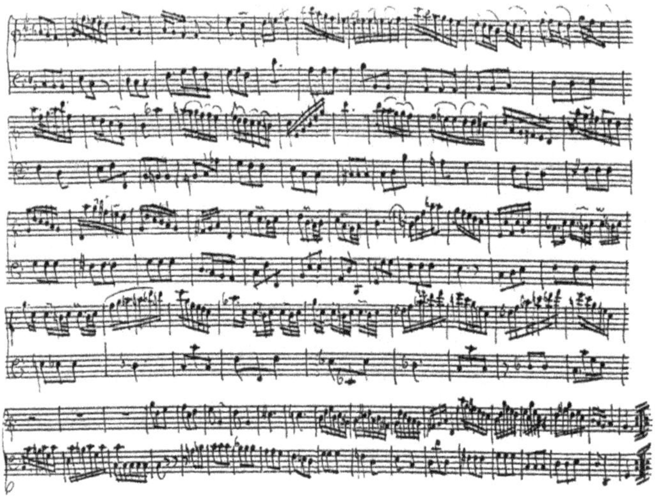

Fig.4: Continued

Fig.5: Pier Leone Ghezzi, "*Sonator del Boè bravissimo che sona al Teatro della Valle nel carnevale del 1751, et à sonato alla mia accademia, si chiama Giuseppe et è venetiano*", Rome, Gabinetto Nazionale delle Stampe, n.2606, c.114, n.274. This drawing shows another example of oboe with the typical straight outer profile from the time and the region of Bissoli. The oboe player in question has not been identified to this date.

Bibliography

Bernardini, Alfredo. "The Oboe in the Venetian Republic, 1692–1797." *Early Music* 16, no. 3 (August 1988): 380–81.

Crosatti, Remo. *La vita musicale nella Congregazione dell'Oratorio di San Filippo Neri di Brescia*. Brescia: Starrylink, 2007.

Frasson, Leonardo. "Francescantonio Vallotti maestro di cappella nella Basilica del Santo." *Il Santo*, xx series ii (1980).

Rizzello, Marcello and Nalin, Giuseppe. "*Virtuoso ben noto, e di molto merito*". *Un ritratto dell'oboista Matteo Bissoli (1712–1780)*. Preface of Alfredo Bernardini Padova: Armelin Musica, 2023.

Tartini, Giuseppe. *Lettere e documenti*. Edited by Giorgia Malagò. Trieste: EUT, 2020. http://www.discovertartini.eu/epistolario/I/224/

Domen Marinčič

Tartini's Music Performed without Chordal Continuo

Abstract: Giuseppe Tartini's violin sonatas have already been suggested as likely candidates for performance without chordal instruments realizing the bass line. A survey of instrumental designations, figuring practices, and formats such as scores or partbooks in sources of his music shows that many of his trios, concertos, and sonate a quattro may likewise have been performed with just strings. Such practices are rooted in a variety of aesthetic, acoustic, social, and practical considerations, evidence of which can be found in other contemporaneous repertoire. Modern discussions have focused on the possibilities of realizing the bass-line on the cello through chords and double stops, but this does not seem to have been considered standard practice. Other elements, especially dynamic flexibility, articulation and tone quality, were seen by many as being more important than fullness of harmony.

Keywords: Giuseppe Tartini, performance practice, continuo realization, bass, cello, harpsichord, organ

It is uncontested that certain seventeenth-and eighteenth-century repertoires would normally, and particularly in professional performance settings, have been performed without chordal continuo instruments. These repertoires include, among others, overtures and dances in French opera, Italian chamber sonatas of the late seventeenth century, Arcangelo Corelli's influential Op. 5 sonatas, and music for bass viol and accompanying bass by Carl Friedrich Abel and his contemporaries.[1] While such practices have repeatedly been advocated for in the scholarly literature, they are rarely adopted in modern performances and recordings; the absence of chordal instruments in any of these repertoires will still be perceived as unusual.

---

1 For French practices, see Graham Sadler, "The Role of the Keyboard Continuo in French Opera, 1673–1776," *Early Music* 8 (1980): 148–57, https://doi.org/10.1093/earlyj/8.2.148; Sadler, "The Basse Continue in Lully's Operas: Evidence Old and New," in *Quellenstudien zu Jean-Baptiste Lully/L'oeuvre de Lully: Etudes des Sources – Hommage à Lionel Sawkins*, ed. Jérôme de La Gorce and Herbert Schneider, *Musikwissenschaftliche Publikationen* 13 (Hildesheim: Olms, 1999), 382–97. For Abel, see Peter Holman, *Life After Death: The Viola da Gamba in Britain from Purcell to Dolmetsch* (Woodbridge: Boydell, 2010), 183. Other instances are discussed later in this article.

Giuseppe Tartini's violin sonatas already seem likely candidates for performance with just violin and cello on account of their indebtedness to Corelli and
Tartini's close association with the Bolognese cellist Antonio Vandini. These
circumstances, along with Tartini's mention of *bassetto* accompaniment in connection to his *Piccole Sonate* and some double stops in the bass line in one of his
Op. 2 sonatas, led to a reference to Tartini in David Watkin's seminal article on
performing Corelli's Op. 5 sonatas as unaccompanied duos for violin and violone.[2]
Gregorio Carraro later proposed that the accompaniment in the *Piccole Sonate*,
which Tartini describes as optional, could also have performed by a second violin,
or that the solo violinist could even have accompanied themselves.[3] Likewise, there
are reasons to believe that Tartini's trios, sonate a quattro, sinfonias, and many of
his concertos would frequently have been performed with strings only. Performing
trio sonatas as string trios falls well within the established performance practices
of the time, and is attested by numerous instrumental specifications on title pages.
Richard Maunder noted that there is no indication of the use of a keyboard instrument in a large majority of Tartini's concertos kept at the Archivio Musicale of the
Basilica Antoniana in *Padua*.[4]

Following Watkin's lead, modern research has tended to associate such practices
with chordal realization on the cello. This may to some extent be a consequence of
focusing on small-scale works, especially sonatas for violin and bass. It is doubtful,
however, whether cellists were expected to fill out harmonies as a standard practice. The modern focus on chordal realization may in part have been responsible
for impeding a more general acceptance of performing some of the concerned
repertoires without chordal instruments. In practice, such performances often
require one to adjust other features such as dynamics, articulation, tuning, or the
quality of sound. These elements were certainly regarded as important by Tartini
and his contemporaries. Neglecting them at the expense of concentrating on com-
pensating for the absence of chordal instruments and completing the harmony can
yield unnecessary complications in performance. Chords and double stops are not
equally suited to all types of bass line. They can quickly become obtrusive, all the
more so when accompanying a flute or recorder, and it is considerably more chal-
lenging to employ them with any consistence in trio sonatas without doubling the
melodic lines in the upper voices, especially when working from separate parts.
Such problems may in part be due to modern aesthetic standards, but they can

2   David Watkin, "Corelli's Op. 5 Sonatas: 'Violino e violone o cimbalo'?" *Early Music* 24,
    no. 4 (November 1996): 649f, https://doi.org/10.1093/earlyj/XXIV.4.645. Despite the
    fact that this article mentions Tartini and cites an example from one of his sonatas,
    this practice was very rarely observed until around 2014, when David Plantier and
    Annabelle Luis started performing and recording Tartini's sonatas as a duo.
3   Gregorio Carraro, "Hidden Affinities. Accompanied Solo, Tartini and Germany," *Ad
    Parnassum. A Journal of Eighteenth-and Nineteenth-Century Instrumental Music* 2,
    no. 22 (2013): 113–26.
4   Richard Maunder, *The Scoring of Baroque Concertos* (Woodbridge: Boydell, 2004), 153.

nonetheless encourage us to reconsider the historical evidence. We may eventually learn to understand and value such practices in instrumentation better if we take a variety of aesthetic, acoustic, social and practical considerations into account. The same music could be, and often was, performed in different ways according to the situation and the available forces. The musicians and ensembles were often the starting point for choosing a suitable repertoire, and we can sometimes be led astray when attempting the opposite by looking for the ideal ensemble to perform a chosen repertoire. Nevertheless, the extant musical material may provide clues as to the various practices of Tartini's time.

While many sources of Tartini's music describe the bass part with the seemingly generic terms "basso", "basso continuo", or "basse continue", at least five editions and eight reprints of his violin sonatas and trio sonatas published in Paris, London and Amsterdam between 1734 and 1764 by Witvogel, Le Cène, Le Clerc, Boivin, Chalon, Walsh, and Hummel specify the instrument in question as "violoncello o cimbalo", "violoncello or harpsichord", or – in one instance – "harpsicord or violoncello".[5] Such alternative scorings had a considerable tradition in both duos and trios, stretching far beyond Corelli's Opp. 2, 4 and 5. Gregory Barnett points out that many Bolognese sonate da camera prints of the late seventeenth century require just one bass instrument, the string trio being a particularly common scoring in this repertoire.[6] Barnett lists 31 sonate da camera publications in two, three, four, five and six parts from the period 1660–1705, 19 of which prefer the violone or violoncello to the harpsichord or spinet. Of the others, six feature separate parts for two bass instruments, while only four of the cited collections give the harpsichord or spinet as a first choice if the bass line is to be played by a single instrument. All six publications featuring music for violin and bass belong to the first group, four of them mentioning no alternative to the violone or violoncello. The distinction itself between *da chiesa* and *da camera* scorings shows that such designations must have been meaningful. The scorings correspond to the different acoustic or practical requirements of the venues – large churches, more intimate aristocratic chambers, gardens, or outdoor terraces. The difference between public and private music making is another relevant aspect in terms of instrumentation.

---

5   The last is found in John Walsh's reprint of Tartini's Op. 1, *XII Solos for a Violin with a Thorough Bass for the Harpsicord or Violoncello* (London: Walsh, 1742), RISM: T 249. This title resembles the firm's earlier publications of music by Corelli, Veracini, Geminiani and others.

6   Gregory Barnett, *Bolognese Instrumental Music, 1660–1710: Spiritual Comfort, Courtly Delight, and Commercial Triumph* (Aldershot: Ashgate, 2008), 45–49, https://doi.org/10.4324/9781315096186. See also Peter Allsop, "The Role of the Stringed Bass as a Continuo Instrument in Italian Seventeenth Century Instrumental Music," *Chelys: The Journal of the Viola Da Gamba Society* 8 (1978–79): 31–37; Sandra Mangsen, "The Trio Sonata in Pre-Corellian Prints: When Does 3 = 4?" *Performance Practice Review* 3, no. 2 (Fall 1990), article 4: 138–64, https://10.5642/perfpr.199003.02.4; Peter Walls, "On Divided Lines: Instrumentation for Bass Parts in Corelli-era Sonatas," *Performance Practice Review* 13, no. 1 (2008): article 8, https://10.5642/perfpr.200813.01.08.

The absence of figuring and the layout in separate partbooks makes it somewhat more likely that the author or publisher expected the music to be performed without chordal instruments. The clearest cases may be those publications that specify just a string duo or trio without mentioning chordal instruments, and where an unfigured bass part is provided in a separate partbook, as in the seven collections from the period 1678–98 listed in Tab. 1. Presenting the music in score, on the other hand, can help performers coordinate and makes it easier to harmonize an unfigured bass line. It can also enable performances on a single instrument as in Dall'Abaco *Sonate da camera*, Op. 1, printed in score with an unfigured bass, where solo harpsichord is mentioned in the title as an alternative to the duo of violin and violone.[7] The same two possibilities, but in reverse order, are specified in Buini's *Sonate da camera* (Op. 1, 1720).[8]

Tab. 1: Selected seventeenth-century prints specifying a string duo or trio, with an unfigured violone or violoncello part provided in a separate partbook

---

Giovanni Maria Bononcini, Arie, e correnti a trè, due violini, e violone, Op. 12

    (Bologna: Giacomo Monti, 1678), RISM: B 3641

Giuseppe Torelli, Concertino per camera a violino e violoncello, Op. 4

    (Bologna: Marino Silvani, 1687–88), RISM: T 986

Bartolomeo Girolamo Laurenti, Suonate per camera à violino, e violoncello, Op. 1

    (Bologna: Pier-Maria Monti, 1691), RISM: L 1091

Giovanni Battista Vitali, Sonate da camera a trè, due violini, e violone, Op. 14

    (Modena: Christoforo Canobi, 1692), RISM: V 2174

Tomaso Antonio Vitali, Sonate da camera a trè, due violini, e violone, Op. 3

    (Modena: Fortuniano Rosati, 1695), RISM: V 2178

Attilio Ariosti, Divertimenti da camera à violino, e violoncello

    (Bologna: Carlo Maria Fagnani, 1695), RISM: A 1421

Tomaso Pegolotti, Trattenimenti armonici da camera à violino solo, e violoncello

    (Modena: Fortuniano Rosati, 1698), RISM: P 1142

Continuo figures make performances with just a string bass no less likely, as is attested by Bononcini's often-cited comment that "the violone will make a better effect than the spinet since the basses are more appropriate for the former than the

---

7   Evaristo Felice Dall'Abaco, *Sonate da camera a violino e violone, overo clavicembalo solo*, Op. 1 (Amsterdam: Estienne Roger, c. 1708), RISM: D 794.

8   Giuseppe Maria Buini, *Suonate per camera da cembalo, o violino e violoncello*, Op. 1 (Bologna: n.p., 1720), RISM: B 4928.

latter".[9] His music is printed in two separate partbooks, and the figures are clearly included to facilitate performance on a keyboard instrument. The bass lines are generally very melodic and active, repeatedly ascending too high for chords or double stops. One can imagine changing them in various ways in order to accommodate chordal playing on the violone, but this would to some extent contradict Bononcini's statement.

After 1700, the distinction between *da chiesa* and *da camera* sonatas gradually became blurred, but a certain variety of specifications on the title pages remained. Some of them may be attributed to tradition, but those suggesting performance on the violin and cello certainly reflect the realities of historical practice. Tab. 2 lists six professional violinists who are known to have, at least on occasion, performed in duo with a cello, viola pomposa, bassoon, or bass viol. The performances in question took place in Italy, Germany, France, and England. Manfredi's partnership with Boccherini is particularly interesting since sonatas of both composers feature occasional double stops in the bass part and, in Boccherini's case, also chords. Such a practice is also found in some of Lanzetti's works and will be discussed below.

Tab. 2: Violinists known to have performed in duo with a bass instrument

---

Nicola Cosimi (c. 1660–1717) with **Nicola Francesco Haym**[10]

Jean-Jacques-Baptiste Anet (1676–1755) accompanied by just bassoon or bass viol[11]

Antonio Veracini (1690–1768) with **Salvatore Lanzetti**[12]

Jean-Pierre Guignon (1702–74) accompanied by just bassoon or bass viol[13]

Franz Benda (1709–86) with **Johann Georg Pisendel** on the viola da spalla[14]

Filippo Manfredi (1731–77) with **Luigi Boccherini**[15]

---

9   Giovanni Maria Bononcini, *Arie, correnti, sarabande, gighe, & allemande a violino, e violone, over spinetta, con alcune intavolate per diverse accordature* (Bologna: Giacomo Monti, 1671), RISM: B 3628, Violone, ó Spinetta partbook, 3: "Si deve avvertire, che farà miglior efetto il Violone, che la Spinetta, per essere i Bassi più proprij dell'uno, che dell'altra".

10 Lowell Lindgren, introduction to *Nicola Francesco Haym: Complete Sonatas, Part 1*, Recent Researches in the Music of the Baroque Era 116 (Middleton, Wisconsin: A-R Editions, 2002), viii, https://doi.org/10.31022/B116.

11 *Mercure de France*, April 1725, 836.

12 Charles Burney, *A General History of Music*, vol. 3 (London, 1789), 675.

13 See note above.

14 Johann Adam Hiller, "Lebenslauf des Herrn Franz Benda, königlichen Preußischen Kammermusikus," *Wöchentliche Nachrichten und Anmerkungen, die Musik betreffend* 25 (16 December 1766): 193.

15 Carlo Bellora, *Filippo Manfredi: La biografia e opera strumentale* (Varese: Zecchini, 2009), 31–33. Manfredi's musical partnership with Boccherini seems unequivocal, but references to joint tours should generally be read with caution as far as duo

These names can be supplemented by general references to such practices by Brossard and Rousseau.[16] Like Tartini and his life-long friend and colleague Vandini, all of the above-mentioned performers are male professional virtuosos. A different, more private social setting for chamber music performances would often have involved a lady at the harpsichord, the most common instrument for a female musician to play, even if some regarded the bass violin to be suitable as well.[17] Johann Friedrich Armand von Uffenbach praises a private performance of sonatas by Corelli and Masciti in duo, featuring an accomplished female harpsichordist, in Calvinist Geneva in 1714.[18] A special situation was that of the Venetian ospedali. The abbé Jérôme Richard describes a performance of violin sonatas by the young Maddalena Lombardini, a pupil of Tartini, at the Ospedale di San Lazzaro e dei Mendicanti in 1762, but without specifying the accompaniment.[19] The performers, their social role and proficiency must certainly have varied, and the alternative scorings specified in printed collections of "solos" or trio sonatas were partly intended to fulfil these various functions. Amateur performances of sonatas without chordal instruments seem most likely to have occurred in a secular setting where, a little later, the incredibly popular duet sonatas for two violins, recorders, or flutes were played. Trio sonatas of the *da camera* or "mixed" kind could be played recreationally with either a harpsichord or a melodic bass instrument, as dictated by the available performing ensemble. If both harpsichord and cello happened to be at hand, both would play, often reading from the same part.

Groups of two, three, or four string players without chordal continuo are a comparatively rare subject in iconographical sources from Tartini's lifetime. Such ensembles are invariably male, are sometimes depicted outdoors, and more often

---

performances are concerned. On 20 March 1768, they appeared at the Concert Spirituel in Paris, but the *Mercure de France*, April 1768, 199, reports that Manfredi played a violin concerto of his own composition, as he did two weeks later, and Boccherini played one of his cello sonatas.

16 Sebastien de Brossard, *Dictionnaire de musique* (Paris: Christophe Ballard, 1703), "Basso Continuo"; Jean-Jacques Rousseau, *Dictionnaire de musique* (Paris: Veuve Duchesne, 1768), 14, 446. Brossard explains that the basso continuo is "often also played simply and without figures [harmonies] on the bass viol or [bass] violin, or with the bassoon, serpent, etc." Unless otherwise indicated, translations are the author's own.

17 John Essex, *The Young Ladies Conduct* (London: John Brotherton, 1722), 84, opines that "The *Harpsicord, Spinnet, Lute* and *Base Violin*, are Instruments most agreeable to the Ladies".

18 Quoted in Christoph Riedo, "From South to North and from the Centre Out: Corelli's Reception in 18th-Century Switzerland," *Basler Jahrbuch für historische Musikpraxis* 37, 2013 (Winterthur: Amadeus, 2015): 243f.

19 Jérôme Richard, *Description historique et critique de l'Italie*, vol. 2 (Dijon: François Des Ventes, 1766), 341f.

than not involve two dancers.[20] The latter two observations correspond to the *da camera* tradition, but it is normally impossible to establish the repertoire. A sonata for violin and bass is quite probably played, on violin and cello, by Achilles Ryhiner and his father Emanuel in a painting of 1757, even if the music in the landscape partbooks lying on the table between them is indecipherable.[21] Their audience consists of the servant François, who listens from outside through the open window. Soon after the creation of this painting, Ryhiner travelled to Padua and took lessons with Tartini.[22]

Two examples may be used to illustrate changing ideas of scoring. We can only guess the considerations behind the instrumentation of Vivaldi's sonatas Op. 2 of 1709. They were announced in the Venetian publisher's catalogue as "Sonate a Violino e Violoncello", but eventually appeared under the title "Sonate a Violino, e Basso per il Cembalo".[23] The sonatas were, in all likelihood, originally envisaged as duets for violin and cello, since some of them treat the bass contrapuntally, use motives from the violin part, and employ figuration more characteristic of a stringed instrument than a keyboard. Another case in point concerns the disappearing distinction between *da camera* and *da chiesa* trio sonatas. Sandra Mangsen notes that certain Dutch, English and French publishers eventually adopted a format with two identical partbooks for the bass instead of a single one for Corelli's trios Opp. 2 and 4, invariably providing partbooks for four players.[24] She concludes that bass-line doubling must have become the norm by the middle of the century. Nevertheless, all four editions of Tartini's trio sonatas published in Paris, London and Amsterdam between 1749 and 1756 feature only three partbooks, and I am aware of no manuscript providing two bass parts for his trios.

Tab. 3 collects the designations found in eighteenth-century manuscripts of Tartini's instrumental music preserved in Austria, France, Germany, Great Britain, Italy, Sweden, and the US.[25] It is intended as a rough outline that may shed light

---

20 For examples featured in the Bowed Strings Iconography Project (https://bsip.org.uk/), see Filippo Falciatore, *Costume Ball in a Salon*, c. 1737–1768, oil on canvas, 77 × 127 cm, bsip 3283; Unknown, *Lady and Gentleman on a Balcony, Musicians Nearby*, c. 1700–99, oil on canvas, 56.5 × 44.5 cm, bsip 3137; Jan Josef Horemans the elder, *An Elegant Dinner Party in an Arcade*, 1744, oil on canvas, 51 × 64.6 cm, bsip 1846; Peter Jacob Horemans, *The Musical Recital*, 1745, oil on canvas, 75.5 × 101 cm, bsip 3666.

21 Joseph Esperlin, *Emanuel Ryhiner-Leissler (1704–1790) und sein Sohn Achilles Ryhiner (-Delon) (1731–1788) beim Musizieren*, 1757, oil on canvas, 182 × 256 cm, Historisches Museum Basel, Inv. 1996.311.

22 Martin Staehelin, "Giuseppe Tartini über seine künstlerische Entwicklung," *Archiv für Musikwissenschaft* 35, issue 4 (1978): 251–74, https://doi.org/10.2307/930859.

23 Bettina Hoffmann, *I bassi d'arco di Antonio Vivaldi* (Firenze: Olschki, 2020), 116. Vivaldi later used the same title specifying the harpsichord in his "Manchester" Violin Sonatas.

24 Mangsen, "The Trio Sonata," 164.

25 In A-Wgm; A-Wn; D-B; D-Dl; D-Do; D-Kdma; D-Mbs; D-MÜs; D-RH; D-ROu; D-SWl; F-Pc; F-Ph; GB-Cfm; GB-Lbm; GB-Mp; I-AN; I-Bc; I-BGc; I-BRc; I-Fc; I-Mc; I-Nc; I-Pca; I-TRc; I-UDc; I-Vc; I-VEas; I-Vlb; I-Vlevi; S-Skma; S-Uu; US-Be.

on eighteenth-century practices. I was able to examine around 550 manuscripts containing bass parts, and every source is categorized according to their designation. Collections containing several pieces in the same hand are counted as one item, but a source may occasionally appear in two different categories simultaneously if the pieces have different descriptions, or when the description on the title page of a collection differs significantly from that in an individual piece. A few concertos survive with multiple bass parts of the same type, but the table only lists their variety and not their quantity.[26] Spellings such as "controbasso", "cimbalo", "obligato", and "repieno" are standardized. The instances without continuo figures are not explicitly marked.

Tab. 3: Descriptions of bass parts in manuscript sources of Tartini's music

Violin Sonatas

No designation	71 (30 figured)
Basso	172 (33 figured)
Violoncello o cembalo	4 (3 figured)
Violoncello	1 (figured)

Trio Sonatas

No designation	3
Basso	39 (3 figured)

Sinfonias and Concerti a Quattro

No designation	1
Basso	15 (1 figured)
Basso • Violone	1

Concertos

No designation	26 (6 figured)
Basso	112 (3 figured)
Basso obbligato	3
Basso continuo	5

26 An extreme case is the concerto Br. D 21 in S-Skma, VO-R [1768] [D 21], which survives with six bass parts, all unfigured: "Violoncello obbligato" (two copies), "Bassi", "Basso" (two copies), "Basso rinforzo" and "Violoncello". This particular source does not appear in Tab. 2, since some of these parts are in different hands.

Tab. 3: Continued

Basso o cembalo	1
Basso ripieno	1
Violoncello	10 (1 figured)
Violoncello obbligato	51
Violone	2
Violon	2
Violoncello o cembalo	2 (1 figured)
Cembalo o violoncello	1 (figured)
Cembalo o violon	1 (figured)
Cembalo	5 (1 figured)
Organo	3 (2 figured)
Violoncello • Cembalo	1
Violoncello • Organo	3 (2 with the Organo part figured)
Violoncello obbligato • Organo	1
Violoncello obbligato • Contrabasso	2 (1 with both parts figured)
Violoncello • Cembalo o contrabasso	6 (3 with the Cembalo part figured)
Violoncello obbligato • Cembalo o violone	1 (Cembalo part figured)
Violoncello • Organo e basso	1 (Organo part figured)
Violoncello • Basso	1 (Basso part figured)
Violoncello obbligato • Basso	3
Violoncello obbligato • Basso di rinforzo	2
Violoncello obbligato • Basso di ripieno	2
Basso • Organo	1 (Organo part figured)
Basso • Cembalo o contrabasso	1 (Cembalo part figured)
Basso • Basso ripieno	1
Violoncello obb. • Basso • Contrabasso	1
Violoncello obb. • Basso • Violone o cembalo	1
Violoncello obb. • Basso di ripieno • Basso di rinforzo	1

While the violin sonatas are almost invariably notated in score,[27] a great majority of Tartini's trio sonatas, sinfonias, and sonate a quattro survive in separate parts with unfigured "basso" parts.[28] Figuring is not a dependable indicator of chordal realization, but clear tendencies can sometimes be revealing. While figures are present in only 27 % of the 248 manuscripts containing violin sonatas, their frequency varies noticeably between the group of sources mentioning "basso" in the title (19 %) and those where the bass line passes unmentioned (42 %).[29] Several violin sonatas with no designation for the bass part are titled *Sonata a Violino Solo*. One possible conclusion is that "violino e basso" was sometimes understood to imply a melodic bass.[30]

Several collections of sonatas are very incompletely figured, but still counted as a single item in Tab. 3. Occasionally, the figures are only found in a single sonata in a larger collection, in an individual movement, or even just in the first line of the opening piece, as in the copy of the Op. 1 sonatas in I-TRc, M 7402. By contrast, all editions of Tartini's violin sonatas and trios published during his lifetime are fully figured, except for his Op. 2 violin sonatas, which are unfigured in both their Roman and Parisian editions, and the Op. 9 sonatas published by Le Clerc.[31] Continuo figures made publications more attractive to less experienced harpsichordists, but, as has already been suggested, opening wider possibilities of scoring must also have played a role. Among the manuscript sources of Tartini's sonatas examined, only four mention the harpsichord, all of them obviously copied from the published collections Opp. 1, 2 and 9. The copy of the unfigured sonatas Op. 9 in I-BRc, Ms. Soncini 181 a-f changes the title from *Sei Sonate a Violino e Violoncello o Cimballo* to *Sei Sonate a Violino e Violoncello o per Cembalo*, which may imply performance as keyboard solos, especially since the word "per" is a later addition, as is the correction of "Cimballo" into "Cembalo".[32]

---

27 Three exceptions where the bass part is given in a separate partbook are D-B, Mus. Ms. 21636/40, D-Dl, Mus. 2456-R-18 and I-Vc, ms. LSM 101/2. Only the last is figured and contains the 12 sonatas Op. 1, apparently copied from a print.

28 While only three of the 42 manuscripts containing trio sonatas have figures, one of these three cases involves just two sonatas in a large collection of 37 trios, I-Pca, ms. D VII 1906. They seem to have been figured at a later stage.

29 To the above list could be added the term *bassetto* in Tartini's letter to Francesco Algarotti of 1750, which implies a stringed instrument; see note 3.

30 Rousseau, *Dictionnaire de Musique*, 446, certainly uses the term in this way when describing "un simple Accompagnement de Basse ou de Clavecin". Note also the single "Basso o Cembalo" in concerto Br. D 32, as preserved in D-RH, Ms. 760.

31 Giuseppe Tartini, *Sonate a Violino e Basso*, Op. 2 (Roma: Antonio Cleton, 1745), RISM: T 257; *XII Sonate a violino e basso*, Op. 3 [sic] (Paris: Le Clerc, Boivin, [1747]), RISM: T 257; *Sei Sonate A Violino e Violoncello o Cimbalo*, Op. 9 (Paris: Le Clerc, [1749–1750]), RISM: T 273. For a list of editions of Tartini's violin sonatas, see Candida Felici, "La disseminazione della musica di Giuseppe Tartini in Francia," *De musica disserenda* 10, no. 1 (2014): 68–70, https://doi.org/10.3986/dmd10.1.05.

32 See note 7 for an example of such a collection.

Some 17 % of the manuscripts containing concertos are written in score or include both score and parts. While all eighteenth-century publications of Tartini's concertos include at least one figured part, labelled "cimbalo", "cimbalo o violoncello", "organo e violoncello", "basso", "violoncello", or "basso ripieno", only about 10 % of the concerto manuscripts have figures. For the most part, they are found in parts mentioning "cembalo" or "organo", some 57 % of which are figured. In contrast, figures are present in just two of 86 bass parts described as "violoncello" or "violoncello obbligato". This shows that many of these designations must have been purposeful. While figures are sometimes also found in scores of concertos where the bass line has no designation, it is striking that only four of the 121 bass parts described as "basso" contain any figures. There was a strong tradition of playing from unfigured bass-lines, especially in Italy, and the differences between figuring practices in solo sonatas, trio sonatas and concertos may partly be due to their varying harmonic complexity. Some of the above-mentioned discrepancies, however, are difficult to reconcile with the notion of omnipresent continuo realizations.

Many concertos survive in evidently complete sets of parts without one that would appear to be for a keyboard instrument. It is not impossible that such parts remained in the custody of the players, whereas the sets of parts were stored together elsewhere. When discussing the situation at the basilica of S Antonio in Padua, Richard Maunder speculates that either the parts have not survived, or that the player used the score, although most of Francesco Antonio Vallotti's works in the archive have two fully figured organ parts in addition to those for cello and double bass.[33] Ceremonial books do not provide information about orchestral music, except for recommending a style acceptable in a sacred place, but the *Capitolario degli obblighi de' musici*, issued in 1721 and revised in 1753, certainly envisages the organist's participation in performances of instrumental music at the basilica.[34] In S Antonio, at least two organs were usually available, and there is also evidence of harpsichords. On the other hand, if musicians employed by the church held an annual recreation in an open-air setting, or any other setting that lacked a keyboard instrument, then the same piece could be performed without organ or harpsichord.

The absence of keyboard instruments would seem less problematic in the many concertos where the solo sections are accompanied by two violins alone, producing a sonority that Tartini eventually became so fond of, but the absence of a chordal continuo in solo sections accompanied by the bass is likewise not unheard of. In the preface to his concerti grossi Op. 3, Charles Avison remarks that the harpsichord "is only to be used in the Chorus", and Christoph Graupner's manuscript parts to

---

33 Maunder, *The Scoring of Baroque Concertos*, 153.
34 Bonaventura Bertini and Domenico Borini, *Capitolario degli obblighi de' musici nella chiesa, e celebre cappella del glorioso S. Antonio di Padova, sì con organi, concerti, e strumenti, come senza* (Padova: Conzatti, Stamperia della Veneranda Arca, 1753).

Telemann's recorder concerto TWV 51:F1 clearly show that the solo sections were meant to be accompanied *piano* or *pianissimo* by the violoncello obbligato alone.[35] There are strong hints of similar practices in Tartini's music. In his unfigured autograph score of the violin concerto Br. D 60, Tartini marks the solo sections "violoncello solo".[36] Witvogel's edition of the Op. 2 concertos omits the solo sections from the figured harpsichord part and leaves the accompaniment to the unfigured violoncello obbligato.[37] The same situation is found in all four manuscript sources of the violin concerto Br. D 55, the second concerto in Tartini's Op. 1. The Largo is left to the violin and cello alone; the movement is absent from the figured bass parts labelled "violone o cembalo", "basso" or "cembalo o controbasso", and the cello part is marked "soli, come sta" or "solo, piano".[38]

The seemingly generic description "basso" is by far the most common term used in the manuscripts of Tartini's music. "Basso continuo", on the other hand, is found in only five concertos. In sonatas, parts described as "basso" are figured significantly less frequently than undesignated parts, while in concertos, they are extremely rarely figured compared to parts explicitly intended for a keyboard instrument. Editors and researchers would thus be advised to avoid substituting the simple "basso" with "basso continuo", since the latter strongly implies chordal realization.[39] Furthermore, substituting "violoncello obbligato" with "basso continuo" in the titles of concertos can alter the perception of the importance and role of the various instruments.

Modern discussions of continuo playing on the cello have focussed on chordal accompaniment, drawing either on sources for such practices on the bass viol or extrapolating from the particularly well-documented practice of accompanying recitatives, which seems to have spread in a somewhat later period and may have originated in Naples.[40] Bettina Hoffmann points out, however, that the

35 Charles Avison, preface to *Six Concertos in Seven Parts*, Op. 3 (London: John Johnson, 1751), RISM: A 2915. Telemann's concerto is found in D-DS, Mus.ms 1033/34a.

36 I-Pca, D.VII.1902/69.

37 Giuseppe Tartini, *VI Concerti a Otto Stromenti* (Amsterdam: Witvogel, [1733]), RISM: T 237.

38 The manuscripts in question are I-Nc, ms. 9965–69; I-Nc, ms. 9970–76; GB-Mp, ms. 60; and US-Be, It. 886.

39 Even the relatively recent Bärenreiter Urtext edition of Corelli's Op. 5 sonatas changes their title in this way, in spite of the fact that the original title page unambiguously states that they were intended in the first instance as unaccompanied duos for violin and violone with the option of replacing the latter with the harpsichord. See Arcangelo Corelli, *Sonatas for Violin and Basso Continuo*, ed. Christopher Hogwood and Ryan Mark, 2 vols. (Kassel: Bärenreiter, 2013), and the discussion in Alberto Sanna, "Corelli's op. 5 and the Baroque Paradigm," *Early Music Performer* 35 (2014): 6f.

40 For an overview of studies on the use of the cello as continuo instrument, see Guido Olivieri, "The Early History of the Cello in Naples: Giovanni Bononcini, Rocco Greco and Gaetano Francone in a Forgotten Manuscript Collection," *Eighteenth-Century Music* 18, no. 1 (March 2021): 85, https://doi.org/10.1017/S 1478570620000457.

very discrepancy between the source situations for the viol and the cello may be telling.[41] The practice of chordal accompaniment on the viol in the late Baroque is so well documented that it makes the existence of a hypothetical undocumented practice on the cello very unlikely.[42] Widespread misunderstandings which have prevented a proper assessment of the historical situation include the unfounded notion that Giuseppe Maria Jacchini already made use of chords in his continuo playing;[43] that Tomaso Pegolotti, writing in 1698, suggests harmonizing his cello parts;[44] and that Quantz forbids cellists to play chords, acknowledging such a statement as evidence for such a practice, notwithstanding the fact that Quantz repeatedly refers to the added notes as ornaments, "Manieren" or "Zierrath".[45]

This criticism is not meant to deny that some cellists would have enriched their parts with figurations, ornaments, chords, and double stops, in accordance with their own taste and proficiency. Besides, things were certainly different in Naples where we find traces of an advanced cello pedagogy resembling partimento practice, and indications that cellists may have been expected to realize figured parts in church music by composers such as Durante and Pergolesi.[46] Apart from that, it is not possible to identify any systematic practice or method comparable to the tradition of

---

41 Hoffmann, *I bassi d'arco*, 505f.

42 For a good survey of such practices, see Bettina Hoffmann, " 'Einige praetendiren gar einen General-Bass darauff zu wege zu bringen' – Die Gambe als akkordisches Generalbassinstrument," in *Repertoire, Instrumente und Bauweise der Viola da gamba*, ed. Christian Philipsen, *Konferenzberichte Michaelstein* 80 (Augsburg: Wißner, 2016), 251–80.

43 This is refuted by Hoffmann, *I bassi d'arco*, 505, but is still cited in Olivieri, "The Early History of the Cello," 85.

44 Pegolotti uses high and low notes above all as convenient metaphors in the self-effacing and fawning preface to his *Trattenimenti armonici*: "Se grata, e sonora non ti sarà l'armonia di sì poche Note, tocca agli Acuti del tuo perfetto intelletto superare il Basso della mia povera cognitione in tal Arte, e così accorderai lo sconcertato in tempi giusti, e sospiri uniformi [...]". Watkin, "Corelli's Op. 5," 649, interprets this as "specifically requesting an improvised chordal accompaniment [...] from a cellist". It is more likely, however, that the passage was meant to encourage the violinist to add double stops. Pegolotti himself provides an alternative version of the last Trattenimento "à corde doppie".

45 This is stated, apparently based on the potentially misleading English translation, in Marc Vanscheeuwijck, "The Baroque Cello and Its Performance," *Performance Practice Review* 9, no. 1 (Spring 1996), article 7: 89, https://doi.org/10.1093/em/caq 030. See the German original in Johann Joachim Quantz, *Versuch einer Anweisung die Flöte traversiere zu spielen* (Berlin: Johann Friedrich Voß, 1752), chapter 17, section 1, paragraph 3, 213 f.

46 Guido Olivieri, "Early History," and Claudio Bacciagaluppi, "Double Ensembles and Cello Continuo in Eighteenth-Century Naples," *Barockmusik, Diskurs zu einem Interpretationsprofil*, ed. Thomas Hochradner, *Klang-Reden* 10 (Freiburg: Rombach, 2013), 185–216.

continuo playing on chordal instruments and especially keyboards, which may be regarded as one the best documented aspects of baroque performance.[47] Francesco Geminiani provides some of the best crafted models for varying a bass line on the cello in his *Rules for Playing in a True Taste*. Besides a variety of figurations, the cello parts in this collection feature occasional chords and double stops.[48] Geminiani's *Art of Playing the Guitar or Cittra* provides an example that may come closest to an elusive continuo realization for the cello, even if the accompaniment also involves a guitar.[49] In the first section of the movement in question, an Affettuoso, the cello part features chords and double stops before giving over to quaver figuration. Notably, only about a third of the notes that introduce harmonic changes are realized, mostly with double stops and typically sixths rather than chords.

Occasional double stops and chords in the bass parts of solo sonatas perhaps give an impression of how cellists enriched their lines. They are found in sonatas by Tessarini, Lanzetti, Porpora, Galeotti, Manfredi, Boccherini and many others, also French composers.[50] Such instances can help understand in which situations and types of bass-line cellists would have added notes, and how often harmonization in a low register was considered appropriate. The fact that Geminiani's examples feature chords and double stops for the cello in addition to the harpsichord or guitar means that such techniques do not rule out the presence of a chordal instrument in the accompaniment. Watkin cites four bars with double stops from Tartini's violin sonata Br. B10, the third sonata from his Op. 4, and suggests that this is not an isolated case in his oeuvre.[51] I have been unable to find other examples, however, with the exception of two isolated moments in the wonderfully polyphonic second

47 Jörg-Andreas Bötticher and Jesper B. Christensen, "Generalbaß," in *Die Musik in Geschichte und Gegenwart*, ed. Ludwig Finscher, Subject Encyclopedia 3 (Kassel: Bärenreiter, 1995): 1194–1256.

48 Francesco Geminiani, *Rules for Playing in a True Taste on the Violin, German Flute, Violoncello and Harpsicord, Particularly the Thorough Bass*, Op. 8 (London: n.p., [1748]), RISM: G 1537.

49 Francesco Geminiani, *The Art of Playing the Guitar or Cittra* (Edinburgh: Robert Bremner, 1760), RISM: A/I G 1564, 40 f. Geminiani's example is discussed in Christopher Andrew Suckling, "The Realisation of Recitative by the Cello in Handelian Opera: Current and Historical Practices," (Doctoral dissertation, City University London, 2015), 98–105, https://openaccess.city.ac.uk/id/eprint/18107/.

50 Carlo Tessarini, *Trattenimenti a Violino e Basso*, Op. 4 (Urbino: Antonio Cleton, 1742), RISM: T 551; Salvatore Lanzetti, *XII Sonate a Violoncello Solo e Basso Continuo*, Op. 1 (Amsterdam: Gerhard Friedrich Witvogel, 1736), RISM: L 638; Salvatore Lanzetti, *Sei Sonate a Violoncello, e Basso*, Op. 5 (Paris: Published by the author, n.d.), RISM: L 645; Nicola Porpora, *Sonate di Violino e Basso* (Vienna: Federico Bernardi, 1754), RISM: P 5121; Stefano Galeotti, *Sei Sonate per Violoncello Solo e Basso*, Op. 1 (Paris: Le Clerc, 1762), RISM: G 138; Filippo Manfredi, *Sei Sonate per Violino Solo e Basso*, Op. 1 (Paris: Fleury, 1769), RISM: M 333; Luigi Boccherini, *Six Sonatas for the Violoncello* (London: John Bland, 1772).

51 Watkin, "Corelli's Op. 5," 649 f.

movement of the sonata Br. e5. Tartini's double stops are perfectly idiomatic for the cello, although it would also be possible to use the additional line in Br. B10 an octave higher as the top line of a harpsichord realization, or to play it on a cello while leaving the bass to the harpsichordist, provided that one is present.[52] The manuscript sources of this sonata are both unfigured, and one of them is written in separate parts.[53]

German writers such as Mattheson and Carl Philipp Emanuel Bach may have expressed dissatisfaction over the lack of harmony when the bass was played with only the cello or bass violin,[54] but performances using just strings obviously offer different possibilities and advantages from those with harpsichord or organ. In 1711, Scipione Maffei praised Cristofori's newly invented *cimbalo con piano e forte* by describing how differences in touch resulted "not only in forte and piano but also in the diminishing and the increasing alteration of sound, similar to what can be done on a violoncello".[55] Tartini's dynamic indications range from pianissimo to fortissimo and include dolce and più piano, but performers would surely have introduced an even greater variety. Quantz writes that "the cellist must seek constantly to imitate the execution of the player of the principal part, with respect both to loudness and softness of tone and to the expression of the notes".[56] In the chapter on the keyboard player, he presents a short Affetuoso di molto, featuring a variety of dynamic markings for the continuo player which follow his prescription for particular classes of harmonic events according to their relative dissonance.[57]

---

52 Both practices were associated with this notation, even if the former is more common in earlier repertoires and especially in solo cantatas. For examples, see Ludwig Landshoff, "Über das vielstimmige Accompagnement und andere Fragen des Generalbaßspiels," in *Festschrift zum 50. Geburtstag Adolf Sandberger* (München: Ferdinand Zierfuss, 1918), 205–7.

53 D-B, Mus. Ms. 21636/40; S-Skma, Ms. C 1-R [No. 11].

54 Johann Mattheson, *Das Neu=Eröffnete Orchestre* (Hamburg: Benjamin Schiller's Widow, 1713), 263–64; Carl Philipp Emanuel Bach, *Versuch über die wahre Art das Clavier zu spielen*, part 2 (Berlin: Published by the author, 1762), 2 f.

55 "[...] si viene a sentire non solo il piano, e il forte, ma la degradazione, e diversita della voce, qual sarebbe in un violoncello". Italian original and English translation after Stewart Pollens, *The Early Pianoforte* (Cambridge: Cambridge University Press, 1995), 57, 238.

56 Quantz, *Versuch einer Anweisung*, 214: "Deswegen muß der Violoncellist beständig suchen, dem Vortrage dessen so die Hauptstimme spielet, so wohl in der Stärke und Schwäche des Tones, als in Ausdrückung der Noten, nachzuahmen". Translation after Johann Joachim Quantz, *On Playing the Flute*, trans. Edward R. Reilly (London: Faber & Faber, 1966), 243.

57 Quantz, *Versuch einer Anweisung*, 225–31. See also Hubert Moßburger, "Harmonik und Aufführungspraxis," *Zeitschrift der Gesellschaft für Musiktheorie* 6/2–3 (2009): 189–96, 204–6, https://doi.org/10.31751/447. Moßburger discusses Carl Philipp Emanuel Bach and Daniel Gottlob Türk as further sources for dynamic shading in continuo accompaniment.

While his discussion is intended for keyboard players, it illustrates both an unprecedented sensibility for dynamic shading and its importance for accompanists. Besides its dynamic possibilities, cello accompaniment also enables greater flexibility in several other musical parameters, such as articulation, tuning, timing, and timbre. In his *Tratatto di musica*, Tartini writes that singers and instrumentalists tune to the organ for the sake of good intonation, but that the organ and harpsichord have no other perfectly tuned intervals apart from the octave. He goes on to praise Vallotti's art and understanding of temperament, but finally describes playing double stops and scales on the violin in their proper ratios, a practice that he also taught to his students.[58] Such intonation of course makes more sense when the violin is accompanied by melodic bass instrument alone and is not doubled by continuo chords in the same range. Twenty years later, Johann Friedrich Reichardt describes how he added chords and double stops to the violin part in his *Sonata per il Violino solo e Violoncello* in order to be able to dispose of the harpsichord. His compulsion to compensate for the lack of harmony corresponds to the concerns expressed by his compatriots:

> This [the full harmony] will give the soloist no little trouble; but how much will he gain in expression if he has a good cellist to accompany him, who not only will not hinder him, like the short attack of the harpsichord does, but will also assist him: for who does not know the splendid effect of both instruments together? What dignity! [...] Just compare this with a stringed instrument and you will notice a very different effect. How much more does the violin lose when accompanied by an instrument whose nature is completely opposed to its own.
>
> Es wird dieses dem Solospieler nicht wenig Mühe machen; allein wieviel wird er nicht auch im Ausdrucke gewinnen, wenn er einen guten Violoncellisten zum Begleiter hat, der ihn nicht allein nicht hindert, wie es der kurze Anschlag des Klaviers tut, sondern ihm auch behilflich ist: denn wer kennt nicht die vortreffliche Wirkung beider Instrumente zusammen? Welche Würde! [...] Man verwechsle dieses nur mit einem Saiteninstrumente und man wird schon einen großen Unterschied in der Wirkung gewahr werden. Wie viel mehr muß die Violine nicht bei der Begleitung eines Instruments verlieren, dessen Natur der ihrigen ganz entgegen ist.[59]

Of all continuo instruments, the cello can best match the articulation of the violin and it certainly complies with the *cantabilità* which eventually became the main aesthetic tenet of Tartini's music. Articulation was clearly among the central preoccupations of his art as a performer, and the poetic texts which are occasionally found under the notes may have guided players towards a more vivid declamatory

---

58 Giuseppe Tartini, *Trattato di musica secondo la vera scienza dell'armonia* (Padova: Giovanni Manfrè, 1754), 99 f.

59 Johann Friedrich Reichardt, preface to *Vermischte Musikalien* (Riga: Johann Friedrich Hartknoch, 1773).

style.[60] Most of Tartini's bass lines may be simple, but they occasionally feature slurs over two or three notes, combinations of dots and slurs over repeated notes, as well as strokes and quaver rests between notes.[61] The Paris Conservatory cello method (1804) tacitly alludes to Tartini's distinction between the *cantabile* and *sonabile* when instructing the cellist to distinguish between accompanying parts and notes where the instrument takes part in the musical discourse. The method cites the opening Grave from Tartini's violin sonata Br. e7, explaining that accompanying notes have to be detached, bowed in a lively fashion, and separated from each other. This is illustrated by notating all the quavers in the bass line as semiquavers with semiquaver rests. The beginning of the final Allegro from Tartini's sonata Br. c2 is given as a contrasting example, demanding a different execution: "The singing notes must, conversely, be slurred, rendered with the particular nuances and intentions of the main melody, the effect of which they must support in a different way, that is to say, by merging with it to form a perfect whole, or by answering to it in imitation [...]."[62] Charles Burney reports that Vandini, on the cello, was said to play and express *a parlare*, that is, in such a manner as to make his instrument *speak*".[63] This corresponds to the description of Tartini's violin sound as that of an eloquent and moving speech.[64] While Burney expressed disappointment at not hearing Vandini in a solo role, this special characteristic, perhaps a subtle attention to articulation, dynamic shading, rhythmic flexibility, and sound colour, must have also distinguished the cellist's ensemble playing. Such qualities would have been all the more important in performances

---

60 Sergio Durante, "Tartini and His Texts," in *The Century of Bach and Mozart: Perspectives on Historiography, Composition, Theory, and Performance*, ed. Sean Gallagher and Thomas Forrest Kelly, *Harvard Publications in Music* (Cambridge, MA: Harvard University Press, 2008), 145–86. The relevance of Tartini's texts for performers is discussed in Claire Genewein, "Vokales Instrumentalspiel in der zweiten Hälfte des 18. Jahrhunderts," (Doctoral dissertation, Leiden University, 2014), 163–89, https://hdl.handle.net/1887/26920. A fascinating account relevant to articulation is given in Pierpaolo Polzonetti, "Tartini and the Tongue of Saint Anthony," *Journal of the American Musicological Society* 67, no. 2 (Summer 2014): 429–86, https://doi.org/10.1525/jams.2014.67.2.429.

61 A striking example for the use of short rests is the opening Allegro of sonata Br. A4.

62 "Les notes chantantes doivent au contraire être liées, rendues avec les nuances particulières et les intentions du chant principal dont elles doivent seconder l'effet d'une autre maniere, c'est-à-dire en se fondant avec lui pour former un ensemble parfait, soit qu'elles y répondent en imitation [...]". Pierre Baillot and others, *Méthode de Violoncelle et de Basse d'Accompagnement* (Paris: L'Imprimerie du Conservatoire, 1804), 140 f.

63 Charles Burney, *The Present State of Music in France and Italy* (London: Becket, 1771), 135 f.

64 "Onde ben a ragione si dicea, che il suono di Tartini era un facondo e commovente parlare". Benvenuto Robbio conte di San Rafaele, *Lettere due sopra l'arte del suono* (Vicenza: Antonio Veronese, 1778), 33.

without keyboard instruments doubling the bass line. A better understanding of the various aspects involved in different instrumentation practices may eventually alter and enrich our perception of Tartini's music.

Bibliography

Allsop, Peter. "The Role of the Stringed Bass as a Continuo Instrument in Italian Seventeenth Century Instrumental Music." *Chelys: The Journal of the Viola Da Gamba Society* 8 (1978–79): 31–37.

Ariosti, Attilio. *Divertimenti da camera à violino, e violoncello.* Bologna: Carlo Maria Fagnani, 1695. RISM: A 1421.

Avison, Charles. *Six Concertos in Seven Parts,* Op. 3. London: John Johnson, 1751. RISM: A 2915.

Bacciagaluppi, Claudio. "Double Ensembles and Cello Continuo in Eighteenth-Century Naples." In *Barockmusik, Diskurs zu einem Interpretationsprofil,* edited by Thomas Hochradner, 185–216. *Klang-Reden* 10. Freiburg: Rombach, 2013.

Bach, Carl Philipp Emanuel. *Versuch über die wahre Art das Clavier zu spielen,* part 2. Berlin: Published by the author, 1762.

Baillot, Pierre and others. *Méthode de Violoncelle et de Basse d'Accompagnement.* Paris: L'Imprimerie du Conservatoire, 1804.

Barnett, Gregory. *Bolognese Instrumental Music, 1660–1710: Spiritual Comfort, Courtly Delight, and Commercial Triumph.* Aldershot: Ashgate, 2008. https://doi.org/10.4324/9781315096186.

Bellora, Carlo. *Filippo Manfredi: La biografia e opera strumentale.* Varese: Zecchini, 2009.

Bertini, Bonaventura, and Domenico Borini. *Capitolario degli obblighi de' musici nella chiesa, e celebre cappella del glorioso S. Antonio di Padova, sì con organi, concerti, e strumenti, come senza.* Padova: Conzatti, Stamperia della Veneranda Arca, 1753.

Boccherini, Luigi. *Six Sonatas for the Violoncello.* London: John Bland, 1772.

Bononcini, Giovanni Maria. *Arie, correnti, sarabande, gighe, & allemande a violino, e violone, over spinetta, con alcune intavolate per diverse accordature.* Bologna: Giacomo Monti, 1671. RISM: B 3628.

Bononcini, Giovanni Maria. *Arie, e correnti a trè, due violini, e violone,* Op. 12. Bologna: Giacomo Monti, 1678. RISM: B 3641.

Bötticher, Jörg-Andreas, and Jesper B. Christensen. "Generalbaß." In *Die Musik in Geschichte und Gegenwart,* edited by Ludwig Finscher, Subject Encyclopedia 3: 1194–1256. Kassel: Bärenreiter, 1995.

Brossard, Sébastien de. *Dictionnaire de musique.* Paris: Christophe Ballard, 1703.

Buini, Giuseppe Maria. *Suonate per camera da cembalo, o violino e violoncello*, Op. 1. Bologna: n.p., 1720. RISM: B 4928.

Burney, Charles. *The Present State of Music in France and Italy*. London: Becket, 1771.

Burney, Charles. *A General History of Music*, vol. 3. London, 1789.

Carraro, Gregorio. "Hidden Affinities. Accompanied Solo, Tartini and Germany." *Ad Parnassum. A Journal of Eighteenth-and Nineteenth-Century Instrumental Music* 2, no. 22 (2013): 113–26.

Corelli, Arcangelo. *Sonatas for Violin and Basso Continuo*. Edited by Christopher Hogwood and Ryan Mark, 2 vols. Kassel: Bärenreiter, 2013.

Dall'Abaco, Evaristo Felice. *Sonate da camera a violino e violone, overo clavicembalo solo*, Op. 1. Amsterdam: Estienne Roger, c. 1708. RISM: D 794.

Durante, Sergio. "Tartini and His Texts." In *The Century of Bach and Mozart: Perspectives on Historiography, Composition, Theory, and Performance*, edited by Sean Gallagher and Thomas Forrest Kelly, 145–86. *Harvard Publications in Music*. Cambridge, MA: Harvard University Press, 2008.

Essex, John. *The Young Ladies Conduct*. London: John Brotherton, 1722.

Felici, Candida. "La disseminazione della musica di Giuseppe Tartini in Francia." *De musica disserenda* 10, no. 1 (2014): 57–75. https://doi.org/10.3986/dmd 10.1.05.

Galeotti, Stefano. *Sei Sonate per Violoncello Solo e Basso*, Op. 1. Paris: Le Clerc, 1762. RISM: G 138.

Geminiani, Francesco. *Rules for Playing in a True Taste on the Violin, German Flute, Violoncello and Harpsicord, Particularly the Thorough Bass*, Op. 8. London: n.p., 1748. RISM: G 1537.

Geminiani, Francesco. *The Art of Playing the Guitar or Cittra*. Edinburgh: Robert Bremner, 1760. RISM: A/I G 1564.

Genewein, Claire. "Vokales Instrumentalspiel in der zweiten Hälfte des 18. Jahrhunderts." Doctoral dissertation, Leiden University, 2014. https://hdl.han dle.net/1887/26920.

Hiller, Johann Adam. "Lebenslauf des Herrn Franz Benda, königlichen Preußischen Kammermusikus." *Wöchentliche Nachrichten und Anmerkungen, die Musik betreffend* 25 (16 December 1766): 191–94.

Hoffmann, Bettina. " 'Einige praetendiren gar einen General-Bass darauff zu wege zu bringen' – Die Gambe als akkordisches Generalbassinstrument." In *Repertoire, Instrumente und Bauweise der Viola da gamba*, edited by Christian Philipsen, 251–80. *Konferenzberichte Michaelstein* 80. Augsburg: Wißner, 2016.

Hoffmann, Bettina. *I bassi d'arco di Antonio Vivaldi*. Firenze: Olschki, 2020.

Holman, Peter. *Life After Death: The Viola da Gamba in Britain from Purcell to Dolmetsch*. Woodbridge: Boydell, 2010.

Landshoff, Ludwig. "Über das vielstimmige Accompagnement und andere Fragen des Generalbaßspiels." In *Festschrift zum 50. Geburtstag Adolf Sandberger*, 189–208. München: Ferdinand Zierfuss, 1918.

Lanzetti, Salvatore. *XII Sonate a Violoncello Solo e Basso Continuo*, Op. 1. Amsterdam: Gerhard Friedrich Witvogel, 1736. RISM: L 638.

Lanzetti, Salvatore. *Sei Sonate a Violoncello, e Basso*, Op. 5. Paris: Published by the author, n.d. RISM: L 645.

Laurenti, Bartolomeo Girolamo. *Suonate per camera à violino, e violoncello*, Op. 1. Bologna: Pier-Maria Monti, 1691. RISM: L 1091.

Lindgren, Lowell. Introduction to *Nicola Francesco Haym: Complete Sonatas, Part 1*. Recent Researches in the Music of the Baroque Era 116. Middleton, Wisconsin: A-R Editions, 2002. https://doi.org/10.31022/B116.

Manfredi, Filippo. *Sei Sonate per Violino Solo e Basso*, Op. 1. Paris: Fleury, [1769]. RISM: M 333.

Mangsen, Sandra. "The Trio Sonata in Pre-Corellian Prints: When Does 3 = 4?" *Performance Practice Review* 3, no. 2 (Fall 1990), article 4: 138–64. https://10.5642/perfpr.199003.02.4.

Mattheson, Johann. *Das Neu=Eröffnete Orchestre*. Hamburg: Benjamin Schiller's Widow, 1713.

Maunder, Richard. *The Scoring of Baroque Concertos*. Woodbridge: Boydell, 2004.

Moßburger, Hubert. "Harmonik und Aufführungspraxis." *Zeitschrift der Gesellschaft für Musiktheorie* 6/2–3 (2009): 187–230. https://doi.org/10.31751/447.

Olivieri, Guido. "The Early History of the Cello in Naples: Giovanni Bononcini, Rocco Greco and Gaetano Francone in a Forgotten Manuscript Collection." *Eighteenth-Century Music* 18, no. 1 (March 2021): 65–97. https://doi.org/10.1017/S 1478570620000457.

Pegolotti, Tomaso. *Trattenimenti armonici da camera à violino solo, e violoncello*. Modena: Fortuniano Rosati, 1698. RISM: P 1142.

Pollens, Stewart. *The Early Pianoforte*. Cambridge: Cambridge University Press, 1995.

Polzonetti, Pierpaolo. "Tartini and the Tongue of Saint Anthony." *Journal of the American Musicological Society* 67, no. 2 (Summer 2014): 429–86. https://doi.org/10.1525/jams.2014.67.2.429.

Porpora, Nicola. *Sonate di Violino e Basso*. Vienna: Federico Bernardi, 1754. RISM: P 5121.

Quantz, Johann Joachim. *Versuch einer Anweisung die Flöte traversiere zu spielen*. Berlin: Johann Friedrich Voß, 1752.

Quantz, Johann Joachim. *On Playing the Flute*. Translated by Edward R. Reilly. London: Faber & Faber, 1966.

Reichardt, Johann Friedrich. *Vermischte Musikalien*. Riga: Johann Friedrich Hartknoch, 1773.

Richard, Jérôme. *Description historique et critique de l'Italie*, vol. 2. Dijon: François Des Ventes, 1766.

Riedo, Christoph. "From South to North and from the Centre Out: Corelli's Reception in 18th-Century Switzerland." *Basler Jahrbuch für historische Musikpraxis* 37 (2013): 237–63. Winterthur: Amadeus, 2015.

Rousseau, Jean-Jacques. *Dictionnaire de musique*. Paris: Veuve Duchesne, 1768.

Sadler, Graham. "The Role of the Keyboard Continuo in French Opera, 1673–1776." *Early Music* 8 (1980): 148–57. https://doi.org/10.1093/earlyj/8.2.148.

Sadler, Graham. "The Basse Continue in Lully's Operas: Evidence Old and New." In *Quellenstudien zu Jean-Baptiste Lully/L'oeuvre de Lully: Etudes des Sources – Hommage à Lionel Sawkins*, edited by Jérôme de La Gorce and Herbert Schneider, *Musikwissenschaftliche Publikationen*, vol. 13, 382–97. Hildesheim: Olms, 1999.

Sanna, Alberto. "Corelli's op. 5 and the Baroque Paradigm." *Early Music Performer* 35 (2014): 4–14.

San Rafaele, Benvenuto Robbio, conte di. *Lettere due sopra l'arte del suono*. Vicenza: Antonio Veronese, 1778.

Staehelin, Martin. "Giuseppe Tartini über seine künstlerische Entwicklung." *Archiv für Musikwissenschaft* 35, issue 4 (1978): 251–74. https://doi.org/10.2307/930859.

Suckling, Christopher Andrew. "The Realisation of Recitative by the Cello in Handelian Opera: Current and Historical Practices." Doctoral dissertation, City University London, 2015. https://openaccess.city.ac.uk/id/eprint/18107/.

Tartini, Giuseppe. *VI Concerti a Otto Stromenti*. Amsterdam: Witvogel, 1733. RISM: T 237.

Tartini, Giuseppe. *XII Solos for a Violin with a Thorough Bass for the Harpsicord or Violoncello*, Op. 1. London: Walsh, 1742. RISM: T 249.

Tartini, Giuseppe. *Sonate a Violino e Basso*, Op. 2. Roma: Antonio Cleton, 1745. RISM: T 257.

Tartini, Giuseppe. *XII Sonate a violino e basso*, Op. 3. Paris: Le Clerc, Boivin, 1747. RISM: T 257.

Tartini, Giuseppe. *Sei Sonate A Violino e Violoncello o Cimbalo*, Op. 9. Paris: Le Clerc, 1749–50. RISM: T 273.

Tartini, Giuseppe. *Trattato di musica secondo la vera scienza dell'armonia*. Padova: Giovanni Manfrè, 1754.

Tessarini, Carlo. *Trattenimenti a Violino e Basso*, Op. 4. Urbino: Antonio Cleton, 1742. RISM: T 551.

Torelli, Giuseppe. *Concertino per camera a violino e violoncello,* Op. 4. Bologna: Marino Silvani, 1687–88. RISM: T 986.

Vanscheeuwijck, Marc. "The Baroque Cello and Its Performance." *Performance Practice Review* 9, no. 1 (Spring 1996), article 7: 78–96. https://doi.org/10.1093/em/caq030.

Vitali, Giovanni Battista. *Sonate da camera a trè, due violini, e violone,* Op. 14. Modena: Christoforo Canobi, 1692. RISM: V 2174.

Vitali, Tomaso Antonio. *Sonate da camera a trè, due violini, e violone,* Op. 3. Modena: Fortuniano Rosati, 1695. RISM: V 2178.

Walls, Peter. "On Divided Lines: Instrumentation for Bass Parts in Corelli-era Sonatas." *Performance Practice Review* 13, no. 1 (2008): article 8. https://10.5642/perfpr.200813.01.08.

Watkin, David. "Corelli's Op. 5 Sonatas: 'Violino e violone o cimbalo'?" *Early Music* 24, no. 4 (November 1996): 645–63. https://doi.org/10.1093/earlyj/XXIV.4.645.

Tartini's Sound Legacy: Stylistic Influences, Interpretation and Performing Practice

Federica Nuvoli

Giuseppe Tartini and Domenico Dall'Oglio: Their Violin Practice Compared

Abstract: This chapter aims to identify elements of Tartini's violin performance practice in the work of Domenico Dall'Oglio, a musician from Padua who is presumed to have been Tartini's pupil and who had a brilliant career at the court of Russia. Of great interest is the study of the sources for the life and work of this violinist, who from being a member of the Russian court orchestra, went on to take on the position of superintendent of theatrical events, festivities and ballets and, eventually, also that of Concertmaster.

Keywords: Giuseppe Tartini, Domenico Dall'Oglio, Russia, Concertos for violin, embellishments, Tartini style

Life

The biographical data on Dall'Oglio are scant and, at times, erroneous or not altogether reliable: in Napoleone Pietrucci's work, *Biografie degli artisti padovani*, his birth is dated "[...] to the dawn of the eighteenth century [...]", and he is defined as an excellent maker of violins and guitars as well as being an outstanding violinist.[1] From recent studies, we learn that we should date his birth to the year 1709, given that he appears to be 11 years old from the data of the census of 8 February 1720.[2] As regards, on the other hand, the conjecture that he was an instrument maker, we know that his father, who was also called Domenico, was a *luthier* working near the Basilica del Santo. Although this case of homonymy could generate confusion, it was nonetheless common practice to pass down the trade from father to son, so we cannot rule out the hypothesis, even though it is not backed up by certain sources.

On Domenico's musical education, this is little evidence: Domenico *père* makes only three of his six children undertake musical studies: the eldest, Domenico, and his two brothers, Giuseppe and Antonio.[3] At present no

---

1 Napoleone Pietrucci, *Biografie degli artisti padovani* (Padova: Bianchi, 1858), 93.
2 Giulia Foladore, "Le suppliche dei musicisti della cappella musicale del Santo di Padova (Sec. XVIII). Riordinamento archivistico e alcuni percorsi di ricerca nell'archivio della veneranda Arca di Sant' Antonio," in *De musica disserenda*, X/1/2014, pp. 35, Muzikološki institut ZRC SAZU, Ljubljana.
3 Giuseppe was to become an excellent cellist, who pursued a musical career in Russia with Domenico and later back in Italy. On the indifferent musical gifts of Antonio, it is worth considering the testimony of Giuseppe Gennari, in his *Notizie giornaliere*: "Antonio, the third, did not go beyond mediocrity in playing the violin, which he plays

evidence has come to light on their training, even though the Swiss historian and musicologist Robert-Aloys Mooser conjectured, on the strength of an article by Arcangelo Salvatori,[4] that Domenico was a pupil of Antonio Vivaldi in a Venetian environment. This assumption, however, is incorrect, since Pietro Dall'Oglio, one of Vivaldi's collaborators, was mistaken for Domenico's father or one of his relatives, whereas in actual fact he was the choir master Pietro Scarpati. From various sources, we learn only that he was a "perfect player"/ "*perfetto suonatore*"[5] and a "young yet nonetheless excellent player of the violin of great expectations" /"*giovane bensì valentissimo sonator di violino et di grande aspettatione*"[6] and that he obtained his first position at the orchestra of Il Santo at the age of 15, as a replacement for the deceased Giovanni Panciera. Subsequently, from 1733 to 1735, he appears as a stable component of the same orchestra. In this period of time, he was in close contact with Tartini, who had been *Primo Violino* and *Capo di Concerto* at Il Santo since 1721 and had set up his own school in Padua in 1727, though he had also been working in Prague (albeit discontinuously) between 1723 and 1726. There are no sources that explicitly refer to a direct pedagogical relationship, but it is very likely that they knew one another, given that they lived in the same city and that Tartini was such a well-known violinist. Nonetheless, the only connection confirmed by the sources is that of a professional kind within the orchestra of Il Santo in the years in which Dall'Oglio had stable employment.

In 1735, Domenico was engaged to join a company of Italian artists employed to bring prestige to the court of St Petersburg for the Tsarina Ivanovna. In spite of this opportunity for prominent work, he remained attached to the orchestra of Il Santo. For in the petition requesting permission to go to Russia, he asks at the same time for his position in the Paduan orchestra to be reserved for him: a request that was repeated until 1743.[7] At the court of St Petersburg, Dall'Oglio combines his duties as a violinist in the orchestra with compositional work: the historian von Stählin refers to him as "an excellent musician and composer"/"*un eccellente musicista e compositore*".[8] Already in 1738, he published his first collection of *XII Sonate a violino e violoncello o cimbalo*, first printed by the Belgian

---

in the orchestra of Il Santo [...]/Antonio, il terzo, non passò la mediocrità nel suonare il violino che suona su l'orchestra del Santo [...]."
4   Arcangelo Salvatori, "Antonio Vivaldi (il Prete Rosso)," *Rivista della Città di Venezia*, VI (1928): 344–46.
5   Pietrucci, *Biografie*, 93.
6   Antonio Sartori, *Documenti per la storia della musica al Santo e nel Veneto*, ed. Elisa Grossato (Vicenza: Neri Pozza, 1977), 137.
7   From Lucia Boscolo and Maddalena Pietribiase, *La Cappella Musicale Antoniana di Padova nel secolo XVIII. Delibere della Veneranda Arca* (Padova: Centro studi antoniani, 1997), 149.
8   From Jacob Von Stählin, "Nachrichten von der Musik in Russland," in *J. J. Haigold's Baylangen zum neuveränderten Russland* (Riga, 1769–70, T. II, 85).

publisher Witvogel, then reprinted by Le Clerc in 1751, a fact that bears out the quality of his first publication.

The turning point in Dall'Oglio's career came in 1741, when he was invited to write the music for the prologue *La Russia afflitta e riconsolata* for the coronation of the new Tsarina Petrovna. On that occasion, he composed music that was enthralling and full of pathos,[9] and very well received. As a result, he was appointed superintendent of theatrical events, festivities and ballets, a position for which he may well have also composed music,[10] which, however, has not survived. Again from the historian Mooser, we also learn that he became an active participant in court life. In his article "Violinistes-Compositeurs Italiens en Russie au XVIII Siècle", Mooser reports that Domenico facilitated the secret exchange of messages between Catherine, later to become "the Great", and her mother, thereby contributing to the court intrigue that would lead to her becoming the new Tsarina.

His career as a musician reached its peak in 1762, when he was appointed Concertmaster of the orchestra of St Petersburg. In spite of this, he requested, and was granted, permission to return to his native country, accompanied by his brother Giuseppe. He was never to reach Italy, however, for he died of a stroke in Narva in 1764.

Compositions

Domenico Dall'Oglio was a prolific composer: over the course of his life, he devoted himself to composition in a variety of musical genres, both vocal and instrumental. He wrote vocal music, as attested by the above-mentioned prologue *La Russia afflitta e riconsolata*, the recitative *Combattuto da più venti qual naviglio* and the aria *E soffrirò che sia sì barbara mercede*, but he was a more plentiful composer of instrumental music. He wrote sets of sonatas (one already mentioned, then a second posthumous set printed in 1778 through the intervention of his brother Giuseppe),[11] 17 concertos for *violino principale, violini 1 e 2 obbligati*,

---

9   Von Stählin writes "[...] the skilled Domenico Dall'Oglio set to music my prologue *La Russia afflitta e riconsolata*, and did so with such a lively feeling for the passions that, during the performance, [...] the tender young empress herself was incapable of holding back her tears." From Jacob Von Stählin, *Nachrichten*, I, 404 and II, 94.

10   The musicologist Mooser attributes to Dall'Oglio the composition of two ballets, *La gioia delle Nazioni per l'apparizione di Astrea all'orizzonte russo* and *Il Pomo d'oro al banchetto degli dèi e il giudizio di Parigi*. From Robert-Aloys Mooser, *Annales de la Musique et des Musiciens en Russie au XVIII Siècle*, I, 133, 194–95.

11   *XII Sonates à violon seul et basse continue*, printed in Venice by the publisher Bartolomeo Ricci. A copy of the collection is preserved at the Biblioteca del Conservatorio Benedetto Marcello of Venice. The Jean Gray Hargrove Music Library of Berkeley also preserves manuscript copies of ten unpublished sonatas. Duckles and Elmer, *Thematic Catalogue of a Manuscript Collection of Eighteenth-Century Italian Instrumental Music in the University of California*, Berkeley Music Library (Berkeley and Los Angeles: University of California Press, 1963).

viola e violoncello obbligato,[12] and a set of *VI Sinfonie a due violini, alto viola e basso, op. I*,[13] in addition to the *Sinfonie alla russa*, which remained unpublished and have been lost. A first interesting feature that Dall'Oglio and Tartini share is precisely an interest in folk music, as represented in Dall'Oglio's output by these last-mentioned *Sinfonie alla russa*, in which he made use of Russian folk tunes. His music was in fact particularly appreciated precisely because it made a rediscovery of this repertoire. The historian Von Stählin relates that Dall'Oglio "[...] had chosen some of the more common folk melodies and, with the various repetitions, he embellished them in the finest Italian taste [...]".[14] It is possible that in conceiving these sinfonias, he embraced certain deep-rooted aspects of Tartini's aesthetic, since we know that the folk music of Istria left "[...] a mark both in certain compositions by Tartini and, more generally, shaped his curiosity for music of the oral tradition, which well accorded with his search, in his more mature phase, for a 'natural' simplicity"/"[...] un segno sia in alcune composizioni di Tartini sia, più generalmente, formò la sua curiosità per la musica di tradizione orale che si accordava con la sua ricerca, nella fase più matura, di una semplicità "naturale" ".[15]

The concertos also offer many valuable insights for assessing any links between Dall'Oglio and Tartini. Moreover, in any research into the influence of Tartini's violin practice on Dall'Oglio's work, one cannot fail to consider one of the most important works written by the "Maestro delle Nazioni": the *Regole per arrivare a saper ben suonare il violino, col vero fondamento di saper sicuramente tutto quello, che si fa; buono ancora a tutti quelli, ch'esercitano la Musica siano Cantanti o Suonatori date in luce da Sig.ʳ Giuseppe Tartini per uso di chi avrà volontà di studiare*, in the manuscript copy made by Giovanni Francesco Nicolai.[16] A further source for our research is provided by specific manuscripts from the Berkeley collection that include certain second movements by Tartini in which a second stave presents the melodic line embellished in the Tartini style.

---

12 The only sources for these concertos are manuscript copies preserved at the Jean Gray Hargrove Music Library of Berkeley, ordered by key and numbered from 347 to 365 preceded by the abbreviation It.; the works are unpublished and devoid of precise references to the year of composition. Duckles and Elmer, *Thematic Catalogue*.

13 Printed by the Parisian publisher Antoine Petit. A copy of the printed edition of these sinfonias is preserved in the Bibliothèque Nationale of Paris.

14 From J. Von Stählin, *Nachrichten*, p. 100.

15 From Durante Sergio, *Tartini, Padova, l'Europa* (Livorno: Sillabe, 2017), 10.

16 http://www.discovertartini.eu/Regole%20per%20violino.pdf

Comparison between Certain Aspects of Dall'Oglio's Output and the Style of Tartini

As a means of studying the stylistic features of Domenico Dall'Oglio's violin writing, I analysed and transcribed his concertos in G Major[17] and compared these important unpublished sources with certain concertos by Tartini.

A first interesting feature shared by the two composers is the similarity, both rhythmically and melodically, between the second movements of the Concerto GT 1.D10 (D 24),[18] belonging to Tartini's first compositional period,[19] and Concerto It. 359.[20] The fact that Tartini's work that belongs to his early period, dating between 1721 and 1735, is interesting because we know that Dall'Oglio played in the orchestra of Il Santo from 1733 to 1735. The very close resemblances in the melodic line of the first bar are reinforced by an exact rhythmic correspondence between the two respective parts entrusted to the violin soloist. There are, however, differences in the choice of accompaniment: while Tartini decides to emphasize timbral uniformity by entrusting the accompaniment to the two violin parts, Dall'Oglio fills out the texture by including the violas and cellos. From the second bar, the music diverges and the two composers develop the melodic material in different ways:

---

17 Transcriptions of the three concertos in the key of G Major are included in my degree dissertation, entitled "Domenico Dall'Oglio e la scuola di Tartini. Analisi di alcuni concerti". For this work, I thank the Berkeley library and its librarian John Shepard, who kindly made available scans of the documents needed for the dissertation, and Professor Pierpaolo Polzonetti, who helped me to acquire the materials.

18 US-BEm, Ms.It.854. Giuseppe Tartini, *Concerto per violino e orchestra* in D Major, D 24 (GT 1. D10), http://catalog.discovertartini.eu/dcm/gt/document.xq?doc=Conce rto_per_violino_D24.xml.

19 The letter D was assigned by the Greek musicologist Minos Dounias, who proposed ordering the works by key in his catalogue of 1935. Dounias also divided Tartini's output into three periods, reflecting the different phases of Tartini's compositional development, on the basis of their stylistic characteristics: first period (1721–35), second period (1735–50) and third period (1750–70). Dounias, Minos, *Die Violinkonzerte Giuseppe Tartinis als Ausdruck einer Künstlerpersönlichkeit* (Wolfenbüttel-Berlin: Kallmeyer, 1935). La nuova catalogazione GT è stata proposta nella tesi di Dottorato di Margherita Canale: Margherita Canale, "I concerti solistici di Giuseppe Tartini. Testimoni, tradizione e catalogo tematico", 2 vol. (Doctoral dissertation, Padua University, History of Arts&Musica Departement, 2010), vol. I, 48–53.http://paduaresearch.cab.unipd.it/3658/

20 US-BEm, Ms.It.359. Domenico Dall'Oglio, *Concerto per violino e orchestra* in G Major, p. 176.

Example 1: Concerto GT 1.D10 (D 24) in D Major for violin, strings and continuo[21]

Example 2: Concerto It. 359 in G Major for violin and strings[22]

---

21 US-BEm, Ms.It.854. Giuseppe Tartini, *Concerto per violino e orchestra* in D Major, D 24 (GT 1. D10), http://catalog.discovertartini.eu/dcm/gt/document.xq?doc=Conce rto_per_violino_D24.xml.
22 US-BEm, Ms.It.359. Domenico Dall'Oglio, *Concerto per violino e orchestra* in G Major, p. 176.

An analysis of the sources – in this case, the Tartini manuscripts that carry an additional stave with the embellished melodic line, on the one hand, and the manuscripts of Dall'Oglio concertos, on the other hand – also reveals other shared features. These include a distinct rhythmic variety, rapid runs that carry the melody into the high register, extensive recourse to the trill and the use of syncopation. While Tartini's writing also presents a partiality for chromaticism, Dall'Oglio makes considerable use of appoggiaturas in the attempt to express pathos.

In order to clarify these shared elements more effectively, I analysed the second movements of the Concertos in G Major identified as It. 359 and It. 360.[23] Between these two pieces, however, there are substantial differences in the general treatment of the instrument parts, both that of the solo violin and those of the accompaniment. In the case of It. 359, the melodic line is simple and unadorned and offers scope and space for the addition of embellishments, to the accompaniment of Violins I and II only. This is a feature with significant parallels in the works of Tartini's second compositional period (1735–50), hence subsequent to Domenico's departure for Russia. It is possible that Tartini had already been formulating the stylistic characteristics at an earlier date and that Dall'Oglio had come across them during his working life with the orchestra of Il Santo.

The second movement of the It. 360, on the other hand, presents a richly ornamented solo violin part, accompanied by an alternation between the Violins I and II and the Cello. The rhythmic variety in this Adagio is also very evident: after a statement of the theme in the opening Tutti, Dall'Oglio embellishes the melodic line with a variety of irregular groups to give the phrases extra vitality, while retaining the syncopated element as a constant feature.

The trill, one of the preferred embellishments of this second movement, is used also to embellish an arpeggio or a syncopation, as well at the close of musical phrases, though always following the precepts expressed in Tartini's *Regole*: "The trill is an excellent thing, and is a perfect ornament in music; but with the same reservation that one has for salt in foods, for too much or too little spoils them, and it must not be used in all dishes"/"Il Trillo è ottima cosa, ed è un perfetto ornamento nella Musica; ma con la stessa riserva che si ha per il sale nelle vivande, il troppo, il poco le guasta, e non si deve usare in tutti li Cibi."[24] Even the use of the appoggiatura to sweeten the melodic leap of a third is an expedient found in the style of Tartini.

---

23 US-BEm, Ms.It.360. Domenico Dall'Oglio, *Concerto per violino e orchestra* in G Major, p. 176.
24 Tartini, *Regole*, 8.

Concerto D39 Re Maggiore

Giuseppe Tartini

Example 3: Concerto GT 1.D25 (D 39) in D Major for violin, strings and continuo[25]

---

25 Giuseppe Tartini, *Concerto per violino e orchestra* in D Major, D 39 (GT 1. D25),
    http://catalog.discovertartini.eu/dcm/gt/document.xq?doc=Concerto_per_viol
    ino_D39.xml.

Violino

Adagio It. 360

Domenico Dall'Oglio

Federica Nuvoli

Example 4: Concerto It. 360 in G Major for *violino principale* and strings[26]

---

26 US-BEm, Ms.It.360. Domenico Dall'Oglio, *Concerto per violino e orchestra* in G Major, p. 176.

An examination of the concertos reveals not only the influence of Tartini but also writing for the violin of great quality and maturity. Domenico Dall'Oglio, a highly esteemed musician in his day, was clearly endowed with excellent technical resources and considerable instrumental invention. As well as offering an example of the extensive dissemination of the Tartini school and style at a European level, he stands as a composer of notable merit that deserves a wider and more comprehensive rediscovery and reassessment.

Bibliography

Boscolo, Lucia and Maddalena Pietribiasi. *La Cappella Musicale Antoniana di Padova nel secolo XVIII. Delibere della Veneranda Arca.* Padova: Centro studi antoniani, 1997.

Canale Degrassi, Margherita. "I concerti solistici di Giuseppe Tartini. Testimoni, tradizione e catalogo tematico", 2 vol. (Doctoral dissertation, History of Arts&Musica Departement, Padua University, 2010). http://paduaresearch.cab. unipd.it/3658/

Dalla Vecchia, Jolanda. *L'organizzazione della cappella musicale antoniana di Padova nel Settecento.* Padova: Centro studi antoniani, 1995.

Dounias, Minos. *Die Violinkonzerte Giuseppe Tartinis als Ausdruck einer Künstlerpersönlichkeit.* Wolfenbüttel-Berlin: Kallmeyer, 1935.

Duckles, Vincent and Minnie Elmer. *Thematic Catalog of a Manuscript Collection of Eighteenth-Century Italian Instrumental Music in the University of California.* Berkeley Music Library, Berkeley and Los Angeles: University of California Press, 1963.

Durante, Sergio. *Tartini, Padova, l'Europa.* Livorno: Sillabe, 2017.

Foladore, Giulia. "Le suppliche dei musicisti della cappella musicale del Santo di Padova, (sec. XVIII). Riordinamento archivistico e alcuni percorsi di ricerca nell'archivio della veneranda Arca del Santo." *De musica disserenda*, X/1/2014, 31–40. (Muzikoloski institut ZRC SAZU). Ljubljana, 2014.

Frasson, Leonardo. "Giuseppe Tartini. Primo violino e capo di concerto nella Basilica del Santo. L'uomo e l'artista." *Il Santo*, XII, no. 3 (1972): 273–89.

Gennari, Giuseppe. *Notizie giornaliere di quanto avvenne specialmente in Padova dall'anno 1739 all'anno 1800.* Edited by Loredana Olivato, 2 vols. Fossalta di Piave: Rebellato, 1982.

Mooser, Robert-Aloys. "Violinistes-Compositeurs Italiens en Russie au XVIII Siècle." *Rivista musicale italiana*, XLVIII (1946): 219–29.

Mooser, Robert-Aloys. *Annales de la musique et des musiciens en Russie au XVIII Siècle*, 3 vols. Genève: Mont-Blanc, 1948–51.

Nuvoli, Federica. "Domenico Dall'Oglio e la Scuola di Tartini. Analisi di alcuni concerti." (Degree dissertation, Conservatorio di Musica "L. Canepa" di Sassari, 2016–17).

Pietrucci, Napoleone. *Biografie degli artisti padovani.* Padova: Bianchi, 1858 (reprint 1970).

Rostirolla, Giancarlo. "L'organizzazione dell'Ospedale della pietà al tempo di Vivaldi." *Nuova Rivista musicale italiana*, XIII (1979): 168–95.

Salvatori, Arcangelo. "Antonio Vivaldi (Il Prete Rosso)." *Rivista della Città di Venezia*, VI (1928): 325–37.

Sartori, Antonio. *Documenti per la storia della musica al Santo e nel Veneto.* Edited by Elisa Grossato. Vicenza: Neri Pozza, 1977.

Tartini, Giuseppe. *Regole/per imparare a suonare bene il Violino, col vero fondamento di saper sicuramente tutto quello, che si fa; buono ancora/a tutti, quelli che esercitano la Musica/siano/Cantanti, o Suonatori/date in luce dal celebre Sigr.:/Giuseppe Tartini/per suo di chi avrà volontà di studiare/copiate da Giovanni Francesco Nicolai/suo Scolaro.* Venezia, Biblioteca Musicale del Conservatorio di Musica Benedetto Marcello, MS. 323. (Facsimile in appendix to Tartini, Giuseppe, *Traité des agréments de la Musique [...] traduit par le sigr. Paul Denis.* Edited by Erwin Jacobi. Celle, New York: Moeck, 1961).

Viverit, Guido, Luksich Alba and Simone Olivari. *Catalogo tematico online delle composizioni di Giuseppe Tartini.* Accessed DATA (ES: 13 January 2022). http://catalog.discovertartini.eu/dcm/gt/navigation.xq.

Federico Gon

Haydn and *bariolage*: An Italian Affair?

Abstract: Although it is a performance practice sporadically present in various composers of the Baroque period such as Bach, Biber, Vivaldi, Corelli and Schmelzer, the so-called *bariolage* (i.e. the playing on a bowed instrument of the same note alternately on open and stopped strings) found fertile ground in many works from Joseph Haydn's output, both symphonic and chamber: in Symphony no. 28 (minuet), in Symphony no. 45 "Farewell" (finale), in Quartet op. 17 no. 6 (IV), in Quartet op. 33 no. 1 (II), in Quartet op. 50 no. 6 (I) and Quartet op. 64 no. 1.

What do the above passages have in common?: the fact that they involved the participation of the first violin of the Esterházy orchestra, Luigi Tomasini from Pesaro (1741–1808). His biography is partially unknown, especially for the years prior to his employment with the Hungarian princes, including a probable period of training in Venice in 1759. One can, however, hypothesize that he studied directly with his fellow citizen Pasquale Bini (1716–70), a great violinist who was one of the Tartini's favourite pupils. This artistic filiation, which is also connected with the apostolic relations of the Esterházy and the Roman cardinal families, could help to trace the practice of the said *bariolage*.

Keywords: *Bariolage*, Tartini, Haydn, violin

Introduction

Among the many effects that can be produced on a musical instrument by rubbing the bow on the strings, *bariolage* is undoubtedly one of the most frequently used and, mysteriously, the one that has had the worst taxonomic fortune. A semantic confusion surrounds this technique, often generating a complete misunderstanding of the real meaning of the term, even among professionals.[1]

---

1 For example, it is completely absent, or treated in a manner that is hardly in-depth, even in basic texts on the historical framework of performance practice, such as Alberto Bachmann, *An Encyclopedia of the Violin, with an Introduction by Eugene Ysaÿe* (New York; London: Appleton, 1925); David D. Boyden, *The History of Violin Playing from Its Origins to 1761 and Its Relationship to the Violin and Violin Music* (London: Oxford University Press, 1965); Robin Stowell, *Violin Technique and Performance Practice in the Late Eighteenth and Early Nineteenth Centuries* (Cambridge: Cambridge University Press, 1985); Stowell, *The Early Violin and Viola: A Practical Guide* (Cambridge: Cambridge University Press, 2001); Sheila M. Nelson, *The Violin and Viola: History, Structure, Techniques* (Mineola: Dover, 2003); Mark Katz, *The Violin: A Research and Information Guide* (New York; London: Routledge, 2006).

So let us start with the definitions. This is the one given in *The Grove Dictionary*, written by a great scholar of organology and violin performance practice such as David D. Boyden:

> (Fr. "Strange mixture of colors"). Term used for stringed instruments. Generally it refers to 1 -a special effect in which the same note is played alternately on two strings, one fingered and the other open, with the result of obtaining a color contrast between the open and fingered [...]; 2 -a passage performed on different strings, to obtain a contrast of colors; 3 -a passage performed in such a way as to play a note on an open string instead of playing it, as it would generally be played, as a fingered note, thus producing a new color effect.[2]

This definition has as its direct source the first treatise that defined the practice, namely *L'Art du violon* by Pierre Baillot (1834),[3] the probable reason why the term has French origins.[4] As anticipated, the semantic confusion is problematic, so much that the same word can precisely indicate three effects which, although similar, are different both in certain elements of performance practice and, above all, in musical result.

That the origins of this practice come from Baroque age is beyond doubt, and the area of origin seems to be Flemish;[5] nevertheless, in the period bridging the seventeenth and eighteenth centuries, *bariolage* intended *lato sensu* is present in numerous composers: among the various examples, we can cite Biber in the *Rosenkrantzsonaten* (specifically, no. 6 "Jesus am Ölberg" C.95, bb. 121 et seq.),[6] the fourth of Schmeltzer's *Sonatae unarum fidium* (1664),[7] or – here given as a sample – the Concerto op. 6 no. 8 by Corelli (6th movement, Allegro, bb. 14–15):[8]

---

2   David D. Boyden, "Bariolage", in *The New Grove Dictionary of Music and Musicians*, ed. Stanley Sadie and John Tyrrell, 2: 25 (London: MacMillan, 2001).

3   "We give the name of bariolage to a kind of passage that presents an appearance of disorder and strangeness in that the notes are not produced immediately on the same string [...]; or as the notes E, A, D are created [...] alternately with a finger supported and with an open string [...]; or, finally, if we let the open note be heard in a position that would require it to be fingered"; (Pierre-Marie-François de Sales Baillot, *L'Art du violon: nouvelle Méthode dédiée à ses élèves par P. Baillot; traduction allemande par JD Anton* Nayence et Anver: fils de B. Schott, 1834), 126. All the translations in this paper are by the author.

4   The *bariolage* is described as a principle, however, without it being analysed or classified, by L'Abbè Fils [Joseph Barnabé Saint-Sévin], *Principes du violon* (Paris: Chez l'Auteur, 1761), 79.

5   Kees Vlaardingerbroek and Michael Talbot, "Vivaldi, Bariolage and a Borrowing from Johann Paul von Westhoff," *Studi Vivaldiani* 18 (2018): 91–114.

6   The year of composition is uncertain; see Thomas Grasse, *Heinrich Ignaz Franz Biber (1644–1704) – Hintergründe zu den Rosenkranz-Sonaten* (München: GRIN, 2007).

7   Charles E. Brewer, *The Instrumental Music of Schmeltzer, Biber, Muffat and Their Contemporaries* (Farnham: Ashgate, 2011), 72–75.

8   Willi Apel, *Italian Violin Music of the Seventeenth Century* (Bloomington-Indianapolis:Indiana University Press, 1990), 235–38.

Allegro

VI.I

Example 1: Corelli, *Concerto op. 6 no. 8*, 6th movement (Allegro), bb. 14–15

These last three examples illustrate a simple interpolation of notes played on not fingered (open) strings within themes that also have notes produced with fingering, and are within types nos. 1 and 2 described by Boyden /Baillot. Perhaps the most interesting use of *bariolage* – and also that closest to the very concept of a mixture of colours – is however the third, which involves the rapid succession of the same note played alternately and, respectively, on an open string and a pressed string, more or less in the following manner, with the different articulation underlined by the different orientation of the stems in the notation:

Allegro

VI.I

Example 2: Example of the notation of *bariolage*

In this regard, a good example is found in Bach, in the third movement of the *Concerto for violin and strings* in A Minor BWV 1040 (bb. 105 et seq.), and even better exemplified in the Prelude of the *Partita no. 3* for solo violin BWV 1006, bb. 17–19:[9]

Example 3: Bach, *Partita no. 3* BWV 1006, Prelude, bb. 17–19

However, if we exclude the sporadic cases mentioned above, the specific type of *bariolage* that we want to take into consideration seems to be very rare even in the Baroque repertoire. The only composer who makes extensive use of it and in a way very similar to the example cited above is Antonio Vivaldi, a fact that may explain

---

9   A very similar use occurs in the Violin Sonata no. 12 in F Major HWV 370, probably spurious; see *Chamber Sonatas. Georg Friedrich Händel*, herausgegeben von Friedrich Chrysander (Leipzig: Breitkopf & Härtel, 1879).

why he is even (erroneously, as seen) indicated as the inventor of *bariolage* itself.[10] Among the various occurrences,[11] see for example, one taken from the *Concerto for violin and strings* RV 315 "Summer" (1725,[12] 3rd movement, bb. 248–250)

Example 4: Vivaldi, *Concerto for violin and strings* RV 315 "Summer", 3rd movement, bb. 248–250

and the other taken from the aria of Arpago "Cinto il crin" (no. 8) from *L'incoronazione di Dario* (1717, bb. 1–4).[13]

Example 5: Vivaldi, *L'incoronazione di Dario*, "Cinto il crin", bb. 1–4

This last example in particular appears in line with the type of *bariolage* on which our research focuses. The next step is to establish whether, and in what forms, this expedient can be found in Joseph Haydn's production.

Haydn The relationship between Haydn and *bariolage* is, if we may say so, a privileged one: no other composer of the *Wiener Klassik* (Mozart and Beethoven included) can boast such a widespread and constant use, in both the symphonic and chamber fields.[14] The broad selection includes the Minuet of

---

10 Such, for example, is the opinion of Fausto Torrefranca, author of the entry "Vivaldi" in *Enciclopedia Italiana*, 34 (1937), 512.

11 An exhaustive list is given in Vlaardingerbroek, Talbot, *Vivaldi, Bariolage*, passim.

12 The concertos were composed before the 1725 printed edition by Le Céne in Amsterdam, as Vivaldi himself admits; see the dedication to Count Wenzel von Morzin; see Cesare Fertonani, *Antonio Vivaldi. La simbologia musicale nei concerti a programma* (Pordenone: Studio Tesi, 1992), 57.

13 Reinhard Strohm, *The Operas of Antonio Vivaldi* (Firenze: Olschki, 2008), 202.

14 In Beethoven, it is quite absent; in Mozart, there are some interesting *bariolage* passages (however, of types 1 and 2) in the solo double bass part within the concert aria (or perhaps an aria written for an unknown opera buffa) "Per questa bella mano" K 612, in the Minuet of the Quartet in B Major K 589, and in the second movement of the Sonata in E Minor K 304.

Symphony no. 28 (1765, bb. 1–3),[15] the 4th movement of Quartet op. 17 no. 6 (1771, bb. 45–47), the 4th movement of Symphony no. 45 "Farewell" (1772, bb. 45–47) and the Scherzo of Quartet op. 33 no. 1 (1781, bb. 7–8).

Example 6: Haydn, *Symphony no. 28*, 3rd movement, bb. 1–3

Example 7: Haydn, *String Quartet op. 17 no. 6*, 4th movement, bb. 45–47

Example 8: Haydn, *Symphony no. 45*, 4th movement, bb. 45–47

Example 9: Haydn, *String Quartet op. 33 no. 1*, 3rd movement, bb. 7–8

Of course, the most famous occurrence appears in the 4th movement of Quartet op. 50 no. 6 (1787), so much so as to provide the quartet itself with the nickname "Frosch", or "Frog", due to an onomatopoeic similarity between the *bariolage*

---

15 This symphony, like many of Haydn's early creative period, has been subjected to various changes in the numbering by scholars. The year of composition is known, 1765, as the autograph states; see Anthony Hodgson, *The Music of Joseph Haydn: The Symphonies* (London: The Tantivy Press, 1976) 202; but it has been labelled as no. 28 (Anthony Van Hoboken, *Joseph Haydn: Thematisch-bibliographisches Werkverzeichnis*, Mainz: B. Schott, 1957), no. 38 (Howard Chandler Robbins Landon, *The Symphonies of Joseph Haydn* London: Universal Edition & Rockliff, 1955) and no. 40 (Sonja Gerlach, "Joseph Haydns Sinfonien bis 1774. Studien zur Chronologie" in *Haydn Studien*, no. 7, 1–2, 1996). Here the classic numbering proposed by van Hoboken has been preferred.

and the animal's croaking.[16] Here are the opening bars, though the presence of *bariolage* is featured in innumerable points of the entire piece:

Example 10: Haydn, *String Quartet op. 50 no. 6*, 4th movement, bb. 1–4

As one can easily see, this typology is exactly the same as that described, with reference to Vivaldi, in the previous section, although in Haydn's hands it is often used with humorous intent and can be viewed as a witticism as much gestural[17] as it is acoustic.[18] The question therefore arises whether such similarity suggests a sort of direct legacy of the Venetian master. In spite of the obscurity of Vivaldi's visit to Vienna towards the end of his life,[19] it is known that Haydn could have had direct access to this repertoire,[20] whose influence – especially in the formal and expressive peculiarities of the *concerto grosso* – is clearly to be found in the first works written for the Esterházy, such as the "Times of Day" symphonies (nos. 6, 7, 8), dated 1761.[21]

However, the common thread connecting Haydn, *bariolage* and the violin school of the Venetian area could have occurred not only through musical sources but also

16 There would be a further occurrence in the Trio of the second movement of the Quartet op. 64 no. 1 (1790), but it does not belong to the type of *bariolage* that is the object of this survey.

17 William Drabkin, "Fingering in Haydn's string quartets," *Early Music* no. 16, 1 (1988): 50–57: 53; Mary Hunter, "Haydn's String Quartet Fingerings: Communications to Performer and Audience", in *Engaging Haydn: Culture, Context, and Criticism*, ed. M. Hunter and R. Will, 281–381. Cambridge: Cambridge University Press, 2012.

18 Gretchen A. Wheelock, *Haydn's Ingenious Jesting with Art: Contexts of Musical Wit and Humor* (New York: Schirmer Books, 1992), 43.

19 Vivaldi died in poverty in Vienna on 28 July 1741.

20 Count Wenzel von Morzin, dedicatee of Vivaldi's *Le quattro stagioni*, was a cousin of Karl Joseph von Morzin, with whom Haydn served from about 1757 to 1761 in Dolní Lukavice, now the Czech Republic; H. C. Robbins Landon, *Haydn, Chronicle and Works*, I (London: Thames and Hudson, 1976), 228–39. The inventory dating back to 1721 and the *incipitario* of 1740 relating to the Esterházy library show how numerous works by Italian composers (Albinoni, Corelli, Tartini, Vivaldi, etc ...) were included in the princely archive, including *Le quattro stagioni*; see Janos Harich, "Inventare der Esterhazy-Hofkapelle in Eisenstadt," *Haydn Yearbook* 9 (1975): 5–125.

21 See Robbins Landon, *Haydn, Chronicle and Works*, I, 555–559; Elaine Sisman, "Haydn's Solar Poetics. The Tageszeiten Symphonies and Enlightenment Knowledge," *Journal of the American Musicological Society* 66, no. 1 (2013): 5–102.

by way of first-hand contacts, enriching itself with a further factor responding to the name of Luigi Tomasini.

Luigi Tomasini The biographical information about the Italian violinist Luigi Tomasini (1741–1808) appears to be very sparse and is obtained from secondary sources. He came from Pesaro, but nothing is known for sure about his life and training. In a letter written in Munich to Lorenz Hagenauer dated 1763, Leopold Mozart reports that

> Mr. Tomasini has been here for three weeks [...] He recognized me before I recognized him, as now he has grown tall, strong and handsome. He was grateful for the old friendship I had towards him in Salzburg, and this touched me, showing me his good heart. He is now going to Stuttgart and Mannheim, but afterwards he will return to Vienna.[22]

In 1757, he entered the service of Prince Paul Anton II Esterházy as a valet.[23] In July 1759, as a result of his outstanding musical skills, he was sent (together with the tenor Carl Friberth)[24] to complete his training in Venice, but he soon returned.[25] In the year in which Haydn was hired as *Vice-kapellmeister* (1761), he was already the first violinist of the orchestra, then led (until 1766) by Gregor Werner. In 1767, he followed Prince Nikolaus I on his journey to Paris[26] and remained in the service of the Esterházy until his death, even after the orchestra was disbanded (1790), enjoying an annuity and appointed director of chamber music.[27]

22　Letter dated 21 June 1763 to Lorenz Hagenauer; see *The Letters of Mozart & His Family. Chronologically Arranged, Translated and Edited with an Introduction, Notes and Indices by Emily Anderson. With Extracts from the Letters of Constanze Mozart to Johann Anton André*, trans. and ed. C. B. Oldman, I (London: Macmillan, 1938), 41.

23　Carl Ferdinand Pohl, *Joseph Haydn*, I (Leipzig: Breitkopf & Härtel, 1878), 17.

24　Carl Friberth (1736–1816) was in the service of the Esterházy until 1776, when he became choirmaster at the Jesuitenkirche in Vienna. In addition to taking dozens of roles in operas produced at the court theatre, he translated from the French the libretto of *L'incontro improvviso* for Haydn (1775) and perhaps also put his hand to the librettos of *Lo speziale* (1768), *Le pescatrici* (1770) and *L'infedeltà delusa* (1773). See Robbins Landon, *Haydn, Chronicle and Works*, II, 58; Mary Hunter, "Carl Friberth" in *The New Grove Dictionary of Music and Musicians*, 5, 251.

25　The prince soon changed his mind about the desirability of this trip, since it was summer, and, with the nobility on holiday in the countryside, neither concerts nor operas were given. Tomasini and Friberth, however, clearly appreciated the city, to the extent of asking for a further subsidy from the prince, who denied it and ordered them to come back; see Harich, "Haydndokumente (4)", in *Haydn Yearbook* 7 (1970), 75.

26　Robbins Landon, *Haydn, Chronicle and Works*, II, 141.

27　Pohl, *Joseph Haydn*, I, 262.

He died a few months before Haydn (who was buried with him in the *Bergkirche* in Eisenstadt), leaving behind numerous compositions.[28]

Why does Tomasini (who is often referred to in the documents, in the German style, as Alois)[29] play such an important role in the present investigation of *bariolage*? The reasons are many, but they can be summarized in two points. The first is that the understanding between him and Haydn was immediately, and always, strong: to understand the skills of the Italian violinist and the artistic partnership with the Austrian master, it is sufficient to look at the Concerto no. 1 in C Major Hob. VIIa: 1 for violin and strings, which bears the words "*Concerto per il violino fatto per il Luigi*" ("made for Luigi", 1765).[30] The second, a direct consequence of the first, is that all the aforementioned examples of *bariolage* were written for ensembles (orchestra or quartet) led by the Italian Konzertmeister, whose importance in the evolution of Haydn's style is beyond question. Just as Johan Peter Salomon cannot be ignored when evaluating both the production context and certain features of the style of the "London" symphonies (nos. 93–104),[31] likewise – and perhaps to an even greater extent – all the quartet collections from op. 9 (1769) to op. 64 (1790) and more or less all the symphonies from the aforementioned no. 6 (1761) to no. 92 (1789)[32] cannot be appreciated without considering the fundamental role played by Tomasini in organizational, technical and expressive matters.[33]

---

28 Including symphonies, 30 string quartets, concertos for one or two violins, sonatas, trios for violin and baryton; see *Komponisten der Fürstlich Esterhazyschen Hofkapelle: Ausgewählte Intrumentalwerke. Luigi Tomasini (1741–1807), veroffentlicht von Erich Schenk* (Denkmäler der Tonkunst in Österreich, no. 125) 1972.

29 He is also mentioned as "Monsieur Luigi", "Luitschi" or "Tommassini".

30 Thus in the autograph catalogue (Entwurf Katalog) drawn up by Haydn in 1765 together with the copyist Johann Heissler; see Robbins Landon, *Haydn, Chronicle and Works*, I, 516.

31 Ian Woodfield, *Salomon and the Burneys: Private Patronage and a Public Career* (Burlington: Ashgate, 2003).

32 The exceptions are no. 37 (1758) and the six "Paris Symphonies" (nos. 82–87, 1785–86), written specifically for the "Concert de la Loge Olimpique" and not for the orchestra of Esterházy. Symphonies nos. 15–19 could be dated back to the years 1758–60; for chronological issues, see Gerlach, *Joseph Haydns Sinfonien bis 1774*.

33 The relationship between Haydn and Tomasini was full of jest and amusement. Well known is the episode relating to Symphony no. 45 "The Farewell", in which Tomasini and Haydn were left alone after the comical departure of the other musicians; see Albert Christop Dies, *Biographische Nachrichten von Joseph Haydn nach mündlichen Erzählungen desselben entworfen und herausgegeben* (Vienna: Camesina, 1810), 41. Another musical game was conceived by the two friends against none other than the Empress Maria Theresia: "On the occasion of a Congress in Pressburg, the Prince Nikolaus had brought his own orchestra with him [...] During one of these parties Haydn conducted a concert in which four amateurs of high lineage also played. The

Crucial to understanding whether the *bariolage* "*à la Haydn*" also owes something to the creative participation of Tomasini is any light shed on the years
1741–57, that is, before he was engaged as a valet. It might seem strange that a boy
taken into service with servants' duties was musically trained. But this was not
such an exceptional practice (at least not at the Esterházy court), and the advan-
tage was that of being able to rely directly on subordinates, for musical services
and more, without having to hire external personnel.[34] However, it can be assumed
that Tomasini's natural gifts, so to speak, had been developed at a young age in
Italy (even if one accepts the hypothesis of a genuine *cursus studiorum* with Leopold Mozart).[35] Moreover, this could be connected with his city of origin, for Pesaro
was the birthplace of one of the leading violinists of the mid-eighteenth century,
namely Pasquale Bini (1717–70), who trained, through the intercession of Cardinal Olivieri,[36] at the Tartini school in Padua from 1732 to 1735 and was held
in great esteem by the Istrian teacher, who considered him a "pupil who plays
better than I do, and I am proud of it, for he is an angel in morals and religion".[37]
Having returned, after a long period in Rome (1738–47), for the first time to Pesaro
(1747–54), he devoted himself to teaching, also playing in the local Teatro del Sole.
Subsequently, from 1754 to 1759, he was director of the concerts and chamber
music of the Duke of Württemberg in Stuttgart, following which he returned permanently to his hometown.[38]

It is not extravagant to suppose that a boy with musical inclinations of, let
us say, 10–12 years of age, could have studied with the greatest musician of his
city. If Bini stayed in Pesaro until 1754, Tomasini could certainly have been one of

---

Empress jokingly declared that she would like to see what would become of the
music if the professionals suddenly left the amateurs alone. Haydn had a very fine
ear, caught the words of the Empress immediately and made an agreement with
Tomasini [...] The symphony began. At the most delicate point, Haydn broke the E
string without being seen [...] then Tomasini snapped his E-string and played his
role well. The symphony begins to wobble a bit ... then it falters, stumbles, and after
a few bars it collapses disastrously." (108–9).

34 Robbins Landon, *Haydn, Chronicle and Works*, II, 35.

35 In whose famous treatise on the art of playing the violin, there is no mention
    of *bariolage*; see Leopold Mozart, *Versuch einer gründlichen Violinschule* (Augs-
    burg: Johann Jakob Lotter, 1756).

36 Fabio degli Abati Olivieri 1658–1738, ordained cardinal by Pope Clement XI in
    1715, was an influential and controversial member of the Roman Curia under three
    pontificates; see Roberto Zapperi, "Abati Olivieri Fabio", *Dizionario biografico degli
    italiani*, I (1960): 24.

37 Charles Burney, *A General History of Music* I (London, 1776) 563; on the same page
    Burney writes that Tartini's favourite disciples were "Pasqualino Bini and Nardini".

38 See Josef Sittard, *Zur Geschichte der Musik und des Theaters am Württembergischen
    Hofe*, II (Stuttgart: Kohlhammer, 1891), 55.

his pupils. At this point, it is important to reconsider the circumstances whereby Tomasini was introduced into the service of the Esterházy princes and to ponder two different scenarios. If the exact date is actually 1757, the meeting between Tomasini and Prince Paul Anton II could surely not have taken place in Italy: at the time (1756–58), the Hungarian nobleman was a general of the cavalry commanding a battalion of Hussars in the Seven Years' War, therefore in the Central European area.[39] It could therefore be that Paul Anton II met Tomasini in Stuttgart, given that Württemberg was engaged in the war (and was indeed a battleground), and that Bini himself was in that geographical area, perhaps with his young pupil. Stuttgart is also the place mentioned by Leopold Mozart in the aforementioned letter as Tomasini's destination in 1763: a city he had perhaps known in previous years, on account of the visit made there by his fellow citizen Bini.

If, on the other hand, the meeting with young Tomasini must necessarily have taken place in Italy, then it should be backdated, since the only known period in which the prince visited the country was the three-year period 1750–53, during which he was imperial ambassador to the court of Naples.[40] In this case, the intercession could have again been due to the *longa manus* of the aforementioned Cardinal Olivieri. The very Catholic Esterházy family (which, in the same period, also boasted two distinguished bishops, Karl, 1725–99 and Pál László, 1730–99) always had exceptionally friendly relations with the Roman Curia, as attested, for example, by the presence in their collections of a well-known painting by Raphael originally owned by Cardinal Giovanni Francesco Albani of Urbino, the future Pope Clement XI (1700–21): the so-called "Esterházy Madonna".[41] Cardinal Olivieri, Bini's patron, was a cousin of Clement XI. Not only that, another prelate of the Albani family, Alessandro (1692–1779), nephew of Clement XI, was the one who proposed the appointment of the aforementioned Karl Esterházy as bishop of Vác.[42] Within this consolidated network of relationships and power, it is not implausible that Paul Anton II could have met the young Tomasini in Italy (in Rome, or Naples, or even

---

39 Herbert J. Redman, *Frederick the Great and the Seven Years' War, 1756–1763* (Jefferson: McFarland, 2014), 393.

40 See Rebecca Gates-Coon, *The Landed Estates of the Esterházy Princes: Hungary during the Reforms of Maria Theresia and Joseph II* (Baltimore: Johns Hopkins University Press, 1994), 44.

41 A gift that reached the Esterházy collection through Princess Elizabeth Christina of Brunswick-Wolfenbüttel (bride of Emperor Charles VI of Habsburg and mother of the future Empress Maria Theresia); see Quatremère De Quincy, *Histoire de la vie et des ouvrages de Raphaël* (Paris: Gosselin, 1824), 12.

42 In 1743, Alessandro Albani was appointed protector of the Austrian hereditary states and, in 1745, also of the whole Empire. Between 1744 and 1748, he also presided over the Austrian embassy in Rome: "The Most Eminent Alessandro Albani proposed the episcopal church of Vác, in Hungary, for the Royal Lord D. Carlo de Esterhazy de Galantha, of the Diocese of Esztergom" (*Gazzetta di Parma*, 18 November 1760, 6).

in the Marche itself, then part of the Papal States) precisely in the period he spent there following his Neapolitan appointment.

Whatever the historical-biographical backdrop to their meeting, it is attested that Tomasini, in July 1759, was sent (together with Friberth) to complete his training in Venice. This period of study cannot have lasted long if, as we have seen, Tomasini is already mentioned in 1761 as a violinist in the service of the Esterházy.[43] On the basis of the possible teacher–pupil relationship with Bini, it is not so unlikely to imagine that the renowned violinist from Pesaro also contemplated the possibility that the young Tomasini could not only go to Venice but also attend, as Bini himself had done years before, Tartini's "School of Nations" in nearby Padua,[44] which was running at least until the second half of the 1760s,[45] and was certainly more renowned and attractive for any violinist of the time.[46]

If we therefore assume this series of relationships and filiations, the hypothesis could be the following: Tomasini, a student of Bini who, encouraged by the latter to continue his studies in the Venetian area, learns – among other things – the technique of a particular type of *bariolage* used in that musical environment since the time of Vivaldi, and subsequently transmits it to the works of Haydn, his colleague for more than 30 years at Eisenstadt and Esterháza. To support this eminently speculative theory there are, however, other details. In Tartini's theoretical writings, no explicit reference is made to this technique.[47] However, a passage from the letter he wrote to his pupil Maddalena Lombardini Sirmen (a precious document for understanding some of his pedagogical idiosyncrasies) turns out to be particularly cryptic – although explicitly referring to the setting of the trill – if related to what has been said so far:

> ... to unite all these laborious particulars into one lesson, my advice is, that you first exercise yourself in a swell upon an open string, for example, upon the second or a-la-mi re [...] to acquire both at once with the same trouble, begin with an open string, either the first or second, it will be equally useful; sustain the note in a swell,

---

43 Friberth was then already under contract as a musician, from 1 January 1759; see Robbins Landon, *Haydn, Chronicle and Works* II, 58.

44 Moreover, Tartini's trips to Venice were frequent and constant; see Pierluigi Petrobelli, *Giuseppe Tartini: le fonti biografiche* (Firenze: Universal Edition, 1968).

45 Petrobelli, *Giuseppe Tartini*, 52.

46 It should not be forgotten that other documented pupils of Tartini's were from the Marche, such as Carlo Ignazio Nappi from Ancona and Andrea Roberti degli Almeri from Senigallia. It was also in Ancona that, in 1714, Tartini discovered for the first time the well-known acoustic phenomenon of the so-called "third sound".

47 I refer above all to the *Trattato di musica secondo la vera scienza dell'armonia* (Padova: Tipografia del seminario presso Angelo Manfrè, 1754) and to *De' principi dell'armonia musicale* (Padova: Stamperia del Seminario, 1767).

and begin the shake very slow, increasing in quickness, by insensible degrees, till it becomes rapid ...[48]

Tartini himself, in various works, uses *bariolage*, although of the simpler type described by Boyden /Baillot (e.g. in the famous *Sonata in G minor for violin and continuo* B.g5 "The Devil's Trill", bb. 190–91).[49]

Furthermore, also closely related to the Venetian milieu are the *Capricci op. 3* composed by Pietro Antonio Locatelli as part of the collection of 12 concertos called *L'arte del violino* ("The art of the Violin"), in which we find once more the exact meaning of *bariolage* used by Haydn. Published in Amsterdam in 1733,[50] they were – by the author's own admission – conceived and performed during his stay in Venice, attested around the years 1725–27.[51] Here is an example taken from the *Capriccio* of the Concerto no. 1 in D Major (bb. 1–4):

---

48 *A Letter from the Late Signor Tartini to Signora Maddalena Lombardini, Now Signora Sirmen. Published as an Important Lesson to Performers on the Violin,* trans. Dr. Burney (London: Printed for R. Bremner by G. Bigg, 1779), 6–7.

49 That Baillot knew Tartini's work directly can be deduced not only from the fact that he was a pupil of the aforementioned Pietro Nardini but also, for example, from the presence, at the Library of the Conservatorio di Padova, of a printed copy of the Sonatas op. 1 by Tartini (Amsterdam: Le Cène, 1734) bearing the autograph ownership note "P. Baillot /Professeur au Conservatoire"; see Juan Mariano Porta, "*L'Op. I di Giuseppe Tartini, contributo per un'edizione critica*," (Master's degree dissertation in music and performing arts, supervisor Sergio Durante, Università degli Studi di Padova, 2017), 28.

50 By Michel-Charles Le Cène; see Rudolf Rasch, "The musical manuscripts in the legacy of Michel-Charles le Cène (1743)" in Rudolf Rasch, "The Musical Manuscripts in the Legacy of Michel-Charles le Cène (1743)," in *Intorno a Locatelli. Studi in occasione del tricentenario della nascita di Pietro Antonio Locatelli, (1695–1764),* ed. Albert Dunning, II (Lucca: LIM, 1995), 1039–70.

51 The period can be deduced from the fact that in 1725 Locatelli was in Mantua, as "*virtuoso da camera*" to the governor of the Archduchy, Prince Philip of Hesse-Darmstadt, while in June 1727 he is involved in a documented performance for the Elector of Bavaria, Karl Albert; see Albert Dunning, *Pietro Antonio Locatelli. Der Virtuose und seine Welt* (Buren: Frits Knuf, 1981), 118–20; Fulvia Morabito, *Pietro Antonio Locatelli: A Modern Artist in the Baroque Era* (Turnhout: Brepols, 2018), 42–44. On the title page of the *L'arte del violino*, we can read: "The honor that I received in my stay in Venice of having been kindly welcomed into your Excellency's house obliges me to testify to you my recognition with this devout office of gratitude, in dedicating these Concerts of mine to you; all the more so since you deigned to come and hear them, and sympathize with them, when, during those celebrated functions, they were given a performance by me with that excellent and incomparably numerous orchestra."

Allegro moderato

Vl.I

Example 11: Locatelli, *Capricci op. 3, no. 1* (bb. 1–4)

This testifies that *bariolage* – the *bariolage* of Vivaldi's style – had not only attracted followers but had also been adopted as a particular exercise in performance skill by one of the most famous violinists of his day, thereby further associating itself with the city of Venice and geographically neighbouring areas, before finding its full place in Haydn's instrumental works. It is only through this widespread use that the technique was later inherited, in the nineteenth century, by a composer who was especially sympathetic to Haydn's work, Johannes Brahms. Indeed we find it, with characteristics similar to those of Haydn, in the finale of Brahms's Fourth Symphony, at the beginning of the Sextet for strings in G Major op. 36 and in the Third Sonata for violin and piano op. 108: further links in a chain that leads up to the experimental music of the twentieth century.[52]

In light of these further occurrences (more practical than theoretical) found in Vivaldi, Tartini, Locatelli, etc., it is not entirely out of place to hypothesize that the frog that is heard croaking vigorously in Haydn's Quartet op. 50 no. 6 is actually a toad born a few years earlier on the shores of the Venetian lagoon and transported overnight to the banks of the Neusiedler See by an expert violinist from Pesaro.

Bibliography

A Letter from the Late Signor Tartini to Signora Maddalena Lombardini, Now Signora Sirmen, Published as an Important Lesson to Performers on the Violin. Translated by dr. Burney. London: Printed for R. Bremner by G. Bigg, 1779.

Apel, Willi. *Italian Violin Music of the Seventeenth Century.* Bloomington-Indianapolis: Indiana University Press, 1990.

Bachmann, Alberto. *An Encyclopedia of the Violin, with an Introduction by Eugene Ysaÿe.* New York, London: Appleton, 1925.

Baillot, Pierre-Marie-Francois de Sales. *L'Art du violon: nouvelle Méthode dédiée à ses élèves par P. Baillot; traduction allemande par JD Anton.* Nayence et Anver: fils de B. Schott, 1834.

Boyden, David D. *The History of Violin Playing from Its Origins to 1761 and Its Relationship to the Violin and Violin Music.* London: Oxford University Press,

---

52 Some of the more recent examples can be found in *Anahit* by Giacinto Scelsi (1965), in the Quartet "Notturno" by Mauricio Kagel (1993) and in the eponymous *Bariolage* (for solo harp) by Elliott Carter (1992).

1965; "Bariolage", in *The New Grove Dictionary of Music and* Musicians, edited by Stanley Sadie and John Tyrrell, 2: 25. London: MacMillan, 2001.

Brewer, Charles E. *The Instrumental Music of Schmeltzer, Biber, Muffat and Their Contemporaries.* Farnham: Ashgate, 2011.

Burney, Charles. *A General History of Music,* I. London, 1776.

Chamber Sonatas. Georg Friedrich Händel, herausgegeben von Friedrich Chrysander. Leipzig: Breitkopf & Härtel, 1879.

De Quincy, Quatremère. *Histoire de la vie et des ouvrages de Raphaël.* Paris: Gosselin, 1824.

Dies, Albert Christoph. *Biographische Nachrichten von Joseph Haydn nach mündlichen Erzählungen desselben entworfen und herausgegeben.* Vienna: Camesina, 1810.

Drabkin, William. "Fingering in Haydn's String Quartets". *Early Music* 16, no. 1 (1988): 50–57.

Dunning, Albert. *Pietro Antonio Locatelli. Der Virtuose und seine Welt.* Buren: Frits Knuf, 1981.

Fertonani, Cesare. *Antonio Vivaldi. La simbologia musicale nei concerti a programma.* Pordenone: Studio Tesi, 1992.

Gates-Coon, Rebecca. *The Landed Estates of the Esterházy Princes: Hungary during the Reforms of Maria Theresia and Joseph II.* Baltimore: Johns Hopkins University Press, 1994.

Gerlach, Sonja. "Joseph Haydns Sinfonien bis 1774. Studien zur Chronologie". *Haydn Studien,* 7, no. 1–2 (1996): 1-287.

Grasse, Thomas. *Heinrich Ignaz Franz Biber (1644–1704) – Hintergründe zu den Rosenkranz-Sonaten.* München: GRIN, 2007.

Harich, Janos. "Haydndokumente (4)" in *Haydn Yearbook* no. 7 (1970); "Inventare der Esterhazy-Hofkapelle in Eisenstadt". *Haydn Yearbook* no. 9 (1975).

Hodgson, Anthony. *The Music of Joseph Haydn: The Symphonies.* London: The Tantivy Press, 1976.

Hunter, Mary. "Haydn's String Quartet Fingerings: Communications to Performer and Audience". In *Engaging Haydn: Culture, Context, and Criticism,* edited by M. Hunter and R. Will, 281–381. Cambridge: Cambridge University Press, 2012.

Katz, Mark. *The Violin: A Research and Information Guide.* New York, London: Routledge, 2006.

Komponisten der Fürstlich Esterhazyschen Hofkapelle: Ausgewählte Intrumentalwerke. Luigi Tomasini (1741–1807), veroffentlicht von Erich Schenk (Denkmäler der Tonkunst in Österreich, no.125) 1972.

L'Abbè Fils [Joseph Barnabé Saint-Sévin]. *Principes du violon.* Paris: Chez l'Auteur, 1761.

Morabito, Fulvia. *Pietro Antonio Locatelli: A Modern Artist in the Baroque Era.* Turnhout: Brepols, 2018.

Mozart, Leopold. *Versuch einer gründlichen Violinschule.* Augsburg: Johann Jakob Lotter, 1756.

Nelson, Sheila M. *The Violin and Viola: History, Structure, Techniques.* Mineola: Dover, 2003.

Petrobelli, Pierluigi. *Giuseppe Tartini: le fonti biografiche.* Firenze: Universal Edition, 1960.

Pohl, Carl Ferdinand. *Joseph Haydn*, I. Leipzig: Breitkopf & Härtel, 1878.

Porta, Juan Mariano. *L'Op. I di Giuseppe Tartini, contributo per un'edizione critica.* Tesi di Laurea magistrale in Musica e arti performative, relatore Sergio Durante, Università degli Studi di Padova, 2017.

Rasch, Rudolf. "The Musical Manuscripts in the Legacy of Michel-Charles le Cène (1743)". In *Intorno a Locatelli. Studi in occasione del tricentenario della nascita di Pietro Antonio Locatelli, (1695–1764)*, edited by Albert Dunning, II, 1039–70. Lucca: LIM, 1995.

Robbins Landon, Howard Chandler. *The Symphonies of Joseph Haydn.* London: Universal Edition & Rockliff, 1955; *Haydn, Chronicle and Works*, I, II. London: Thames and Hudson, 1976.

Sisiman, Elaine. "Haydn's Solar Poetics. The Tageszeiten Symphonies and Enlightenment Knowledge". *Journal of the American Musicological Society* 66, no. 1 (2013): 5–102.

Sittard, Josef. *Zur Geschichte der Musik und des Theaters am Württembergischen Hofe*, II. Stuttgard: Kohlhammer, 1891.

Stowell, Robin. *Violin Technique and Performance Practice in the Late Eighteenth and Early Nineteenth Centuries.* Cambridge: Cambridge University Press, 1985; *The Early Violin and Viola: A Pratical Guide.* Cambridge: Cambridge University Press, 2001.

Strohm, Reinhard. *The Operas of Antonio Vivaldi.* Firenze: Olschki, 2008.

The Letters of Mozart & His Family di lui, Chronologically Arranged, Translated and Edited with an Introduction, Notes and Indices by Emily Anderson; with Extracts from the Letters of Constanze Mozart to Johann Anton André, Translated and Edited by C. B. Oldman, I. London: Macmillan, 1938.

Van Hoboken, Anthony. *Joseph Haydn: Thematisch-bibliographisches Werkverzeichnis.* Mainz: B. Schott, 1957.

Vlaardingerbroek, Kees and Michael Talbot. "Vivaldi, Bariolage and a Borrowing from Johann Paul von Westhoff". *Studi Vivaldiani* 18 (2018). 91–114.

Wheelock, Gretchen A. *Haydns Ingenious Jesting with Art: Contexts of Musical wit and Humor.* New York: Schirmer Books, 1992.

Woodfield, Ian. *Salomon and the Burneys: Private Patronage and a Public Career.*
Burlington: Ashgate, 2003.

Zapperi, Roberto. "Abati Olivieri Fabio". *Dizionario biografico degli italiani,* I
(1960).

Scores

Bach, Johann Sebastian. *"Partita no. 3" BWV 1006.* München: Henle Verlag, 2009.

Biber, Franz Ignaz von. *"Rosenkrantzsonaten no. 6" C.95.* Bad Reichenal: Comes
Verlag, 1990.

Carter, Elliott. *Bariolage.* London, Boosey&Hawkes, 1992.

Corelli, Arcangelo. *Concerto grosso op. 6 no. 8.* Milano: Carish, 1937.

Haydn, Franz Joseph. *String Quartet op. 33 no. 1.* München: Henle Verlag, 2004.

Haydn, Franz Joseph. *String Quartet op. 17 no. 6.* München: Henle Verlag, 2006.

Haydn, Franz Joseph. *Symphony no. 28.* München: Henle Verlag, 2008.

Haydn, Franz Joseph. *String Quartet op. 50 no. 6.* München: Henle Verlag, 2009.

Haydn, Franz Joseph. *Symphony no. 45.* München: Henle Verlag, 2012.

Locatelli, Antonio. *Capricci op. 3, no. 1.* Amsterdam: Groen, 1981.

Scelsi, Giacinto. *Anahit.* Salabert: EAS, 1968.

Schmeltzer, Johann Heinrich. *Sonatae unarum fidium.* Vienna: Universal, 2010.

Tartini, Giuseppe. *"Sonata in G minor for violin and continuo" B.g5.*
Milano: Ricordi, 1920.

Vivaldi, Antonio. *"Concerto for violin and strings" RV 315.* Milano: Ricordi, 1950.

Vivaldi, Antonio. *L'incoronazione di Dario.* Torino: Biblioteca Nazionale
Universitaria, (I-Tn): Giordano 38.

Dario Marušić

Folk Fiddling in Istria

Abstract: The instrumental folk music of northern Istria is characterized mainly by the groups known as *Gunjci*, the core of which is a fiddle and a small double bass. The Gunjci repertoire consisted of dances as well as wedding and carnival marches. Certain stylistic, organological and terminological features of this tradition connect us to the Baroque era. A clear link between Tartini and Istrian folk music, however, still remains only a matter of guesswork.

Keywords: Gunjci, viulin, bajs, partida, Istria, Venice

The instrumental folk music of northern Istria is most certainly transnational in nature. In other words, Croats, Italians and Slovenes share an almost identical instrumental and dance repertoire, which differs from place to place only in the frequency of certain melodies. The reasons for this situation are not only the mutual exchanges but also certain shared non-Istrian influences. In a historical sense, the instrumental tradition of northern Istria is characterized mainly by the groups known as *Gunjci* (but also *Pišćaci, Zigozaini, Zingelci*), the core of which consists of a fiddle and a two-string small double bass.

The contacts between Northern Istria and Friuli are ancient, and the Friulian influence on Istrian musical traditions is significant. Certain writers of the past[1] assume that the massive use of fiddle and bass was introduced by traveling musicians who came from Carnia and Friuli. Over the course of time, these musicians were increasingly invited to play at the weddings of richer families, and the frequent presence of these groups introduced a new aesthetic, especially with new repertoire, though using instruments known in Istria (the fiddle was documented already in the seventeenth century). All of this led to the creation of similar local groups.

Today the Gunjci are still to be found in the regions of Buzet and Buje, whereas in the past, they were much wider spread. In the twentieth century, their presence was documented in about 70 localities. We know that in at least 50 of them there were local musicians.[2]

The *fiddles* (*viulin, škant, picio zighizun, zinglić, mala gigla*) were mostly purchased instruments of non-Istrian origin (for the most part made in Trieste and Bohemia), but some are also the products of local makers. Often one

---

1   Antonio Facchinetti, *Degli Slavi istriani* (L'Istria, 1847); Giuseppe Vidossi, *Saggi e Scritti Minori di Folklore* (Torino: Bottega d'Erasmo, 1960), 30–36.

2   Roberto Starec, *Strumenti e suonatori in Istria* (Udine: Pizzicato 1990).

notices adaptations and the replacement of certain parts such as the bridge, nuts and soundpost. On some factory-made fiddles, the original neck has been replaced with a new one attached in the style of Baroque instruments, and certain homemade fiddles have a flat back. The bows are usually common violin bows, though sometimes a shorter and heavier homemade bow is used for the second fiddle.

Although different from an organological point of view, it is worth mentioning the reed fiddle (*viulin ut kanele, viulin de cana*). It is in fact an Arundo donax tube with two strings mounted. Instead of a bow, a sorghum stick coated with rosin is used to play. Many musicians started to learn the repertoire on such an instrument in their childhood.

The Istrian small bass (*bajs, bajsadur, leron, grando zighizun, vela gigla*) is an instrument with dimensions ranging from those of a small bass to a cello. Like the fiddles, *bajs* have different origins: they were bought by Cargneli[3] and Roma-travelling musicians, purchased in Trieste and Bohemia or, not rarely, also made in Istria. Istrian bajs have only two gut strings tuned in fifths or (rarely) in fourths. This was also the case on instruments originally built with three or four strings. Certain bajses were hollowed out of a tree trunk so that the neck, back and sides were made from a single piece. The most interesting feature of the bajs is the shape of the bridge. In fact, the instrument does not have a soundpost in the true sense; instead, this role is taken over by one foot of the bridge, which is longer and rests on the bottom of the instrument through a rectangular opening in the soundboard. This interesting bridge shape is not exclusively an Istrian peculiarity; it is also found in Poland and Slovakia. There are also bass instruments with this feature in the Castello Principesco of Merano and in Carnia.[4]

3   The inhabitants of Carnia.
4   This kind of bridge is documented in the sixteenth century in a painting exhibited in Goldegg Castle in Austria (1536) and also depicted in the *Reutterliedlin* printed in Frankfurt am Main (1535). http://vihueladearco.blogspot.com/2008/07/treble-vihuela-de-arco-based-on-goldegg.html

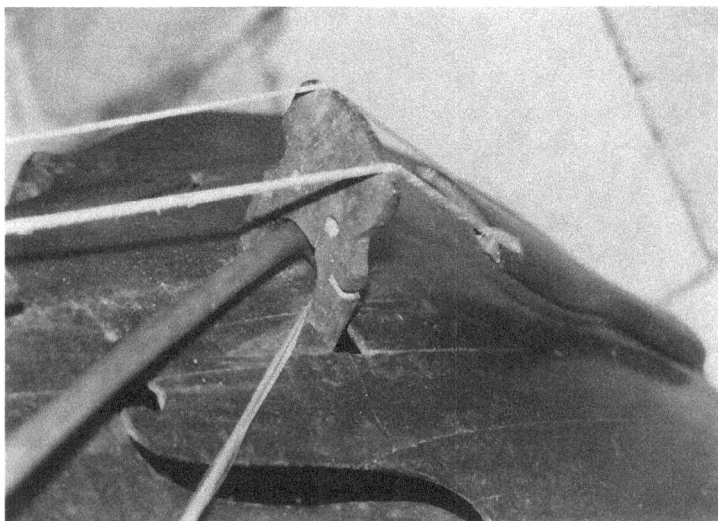

Fig. 1: Detail of the bajs bridge (1990)

The fiddlers hold the neck of the instrument in the palm of their hand between thumb and forefinger, with the wrists pressing against the ribs. The fiddle rests on the musician's clavicle or, even lower, against the chest. Most of the fiddlers use mainly three fingers in the first position. Vibrato is not very common, but it is always executed by alternating different pressures on the string (as Tartini says: "*alzando un poco il dito dalla corda*"). We must bear in mind that this and few other ornaments are improvised during performance. As each da capo is a variation, diminution is the basic way to make the changes. The older fiddlers always used to play on double strings, with the open string as a drone, but in certain tunes some also use genuine double stops. When we started our research at the beginning of the 1970s, the use of double strings was still almost the rule, and the second fiddle played the accompaniment in the manner of a *šekundivanje* (rhythmic accompaniment) or *kompjamento* (fulfilment). The second fiddle would rest with the ribs upright on the left or right shoulder, or on the chest under the chin. Not so commonly, a viola was also used instead of the second fiddle.

Fig. 2: Gunjci. Bajs, second fiddle, first fiddle (1970)

The Gunjci repertoire consists (or consisted) of dances as well as wedding and carnival marches. Because of present-day dancers, only polkas and waltzes are still performed, so a few of the older tunes like the *cotić* or *bašovien* were adapted to those dances. The *arie*, or tunes in rubato rhythm played in front of the bride's house, were already beginning to disappear in the 1940s.

The structure of the compositions is based on the alternation of the keys of the tonic and dominant or dominant and subdominant. The number of repetitions is not strictly defined but is usually uneven, and the piece ends in the original key with the addition of a coda (*la longa, na dugo*). The prevailing scales are not only major but also Lydian and Mixolydian. Older bajs players accompany the tunes with rhythmic drones or use two-or four-beat *basso ostinato* modules, while the younger are influenced by the bass instruments of the brass bands. Certain Gunjci introduced the clarinet quite early in the nineteenth century.

The musicians were almost all amateurs or semi-professionals. Opportunities for better earnings were weddings and dance parties where the dances were auctioned. It is interesting that the auctioned dances in northern Istria were not individual dances but consisted of a suite, and the suite was called a *partida*.

With the advent of brass music, the basics of music theory began to spread throughout the villages. In most cases, only the bandmaster was musically trained, while the rest played according to his instructions. Each player was given his part, from which he was not allowed to deviate. This unification set new aesthetic standards, in contrast to the earlier relative freedom of individual interpretation. Among the people only the brass music was still considered to be "real" music, while fiddlers and bajs players became merely "those who play in the old-fashioned way". The reason for abandoning the fiddle should also be sought in the arrival of the diatonic accordion, which started to play a leading role in folk music. With the modernity of the accordion, an economic factor also prevailed. After all, the accordionist could perform alone, in contrast to the previous minimum requirement of at least two musicians. As a result, many fiddlers simply switched to the accordion.

Another problem was the introduction of new keys and types of modulation, which some fiddlers tried to solve by not always successfully retuning the instrument. Hence the fiddler became just an optional member of the group, and in this context, the old fiddle technique failed to continue. The more authentic fiddlers are still today those who continue to play the instrument out of personal choice in an "old-fashioned" modal style either in a small group or alone. Ultimately, the disappearance of the Gunjci was also influenced by post-War events, which led to abundant emigration, especially from the Buje region.

For most of today's groups, we can only conditionally say that they are Gunjci; instead, we could define them as generic "folk bands" with only the bajs included in the ensemble.

Concerning the links between Tartini and Istrian folk music, we really wonder how much opportunity the young Tartini had to listen to and observe folk musicians and singers during his Istrian childhood. It is true that we find folk melodies in his music. And given that he says that he paid his fee to those blind violinists in Venice because he learned from them too, this is the most concrete trace we have of his interest in violin folk music. Our opinion, however, is that it would be worth looking for those influences first of all in the Veneto area.

We also find it risky to speculate on the two-part polyphony of Istrian descant because as far as we know about Istrian descants today, there is no evidence that they would have ever been present outside the Istriot[5] linguistic zone of southern Istria, and the young Tartini hardly travelled that far. Similar musical styles, however, existed until recent times in the Marche and Umbria regions, and traces have also been found in Romagna and in the Venetian lagoon.

Concerning the Dalmatian nation, "whose music has no specific intervals",[6] Tartini may have come into contact with Dalmatians either in Ancona, as it was one of the most important ports for ships coming from Dalmatia, or in Assisi, through meetings with certain pilgrims; or even in Venice among the large Schiavonian (mostly Dalmatian) community. However, it is also true that there is a

---

5   Istriot is the Romance language still spoken in the southwestern part of Istria.
6   Giuseppe Tartini, *Trattato di musica secondo la vera scienza dell'armonia* (Padova: Stamperia del Seminario, 1754, 151): "[...] la odierna Dalmata Nazione, la di cui musica non ha intervalli determinati, ma è un continuo di voce protratto a discrezione, in grave, e acuto."

possibility that the young Tartini came into contact with the melodies of the Slavic liturgy at the Glagolitic monastery in Koper/Capodistria.

In conclusion, we may say that until at least some melody is identified as explicitly derived from Istrian repertoires, everything else is potentially fascinating, but still remains only guesswork.

Bibliography

Facchinetti, Antonio. "Degli Slavi istriani." *L'Istria, anno II,* no. 21–27 (1847): 81–89, 93–100, 102–6.

Starec, Roberto. *Strumenti e suonatori in Istria.* Udine: Pizzicato, 1990.

Tartini, Giuseppe. *Trattato di musica secondo la vera scienza dell'armonia.* Padova: Stamperia del Seminario, 1754.

Vidossi, Giuseppe. *Saggi e Scritti Minori di Folklore,* 30–36. Torino: Bottega d'Erasmo, 1960. https://dariomarusic.com/

Index of Names

www.ingramcontent.com/pod-product-compliance
Lightning Source LLC
Chambersburg PA
CBHW030244100426
42812CB00002B/312